J 03
Pla
A wo

$25.00
ocn969378245
First U.S. edition.

A WORLD OF INFORMATION

JAMES BROWN & RICHARD PLATT

CANDLEWICK STUDIO

A WORLD of INFORMATION

Contents

DIFFERENT TYPES of
K N O T S

There are countless ways to tie rope, but most give you different versions of a small number of useful knots. The days when each trade had its own knots are past, but knots haven't lost their beauty or charm — and they still have some surprising uses.

When sailing ships were worlds of rope, sailors were masters of knots and wrote about them as early as the seventeenth century. Landsmen used knots, too; many were unique, but the same knot often appeared in different guises. The "clove hitch," which sailors used to make rope steps for climbing the rigging, was the "builder's knot" on construction sites. To circus roustabouts, it was the "dry-weather hitch" because rain made it difficult to untie. Decorators, archers, millers, netmakers, hunters, and fishermen all had their own names for this knot.

BAKER'S KNOT
You don't need rope or string to tie a knot: soft bakery dough will do. Tied in an "overhand" knot, then sprinkled with sesame seeds or salt and baked, dough becomes a tasty pretzel.

MODEST SPECIALISTS

The simplicity of a knot can hide sophistication. Fishing line, for instance, is made of slippery nylon, so anglers can't use many of the knots that work in rope, but the "fisherman's knot" ties it securely.

The "bowline" is a favorite with rock climbers. Pulling on the loop of the knot always loosens it, which makes it easy to undo in a hurry. But this also means there's a chance it will come loose accidentally, so climbers tend to fix the bowline in place with an "overhand" knot. This knot is so simple that, with a little practice, it can be tied one-handed. Yet it grasps the rope tightly and makes the perfect "stopper," preventing a loose end from running through a pulley.

The "sheepshank" had a macabre use at sea: it was essential for swift yardarm hangings.

For the Inca people of Peru, knots on cords called quipus were the only way to record numbers.

TYING A PUZZLE
Grasp one end of a piece of rope in your left hand, and the other end in your right. Now tie a knot in the rope without letting go with either hand. Impossible? Not if you know the secret! Turn the book upside down to find it.

ANSWER: Fold your arms before gripping the rope — then unfold them.

KNOTS AND MATH

There's more to knots than securing shoelaces, circus tents, and condemned men. Mathematicians studied knots in the 1880s, after the eminent Irish scientist Lord Kelvin (1824–1907) suggested that chemical elements (see pages 44–45) might be knots in the "ether," a gas-like substance that he believed filled the universe. The knot theory that he pioneered classified knots by the number of times the rope crossed. The discovery of atomic particles some thirty years later provided a better explanation of the elements, and Kelvin's theory was mostly forgotten. But he had the last laugh: today, knot theory is used in all kinds of things, from the study of DNA to quantum computing.

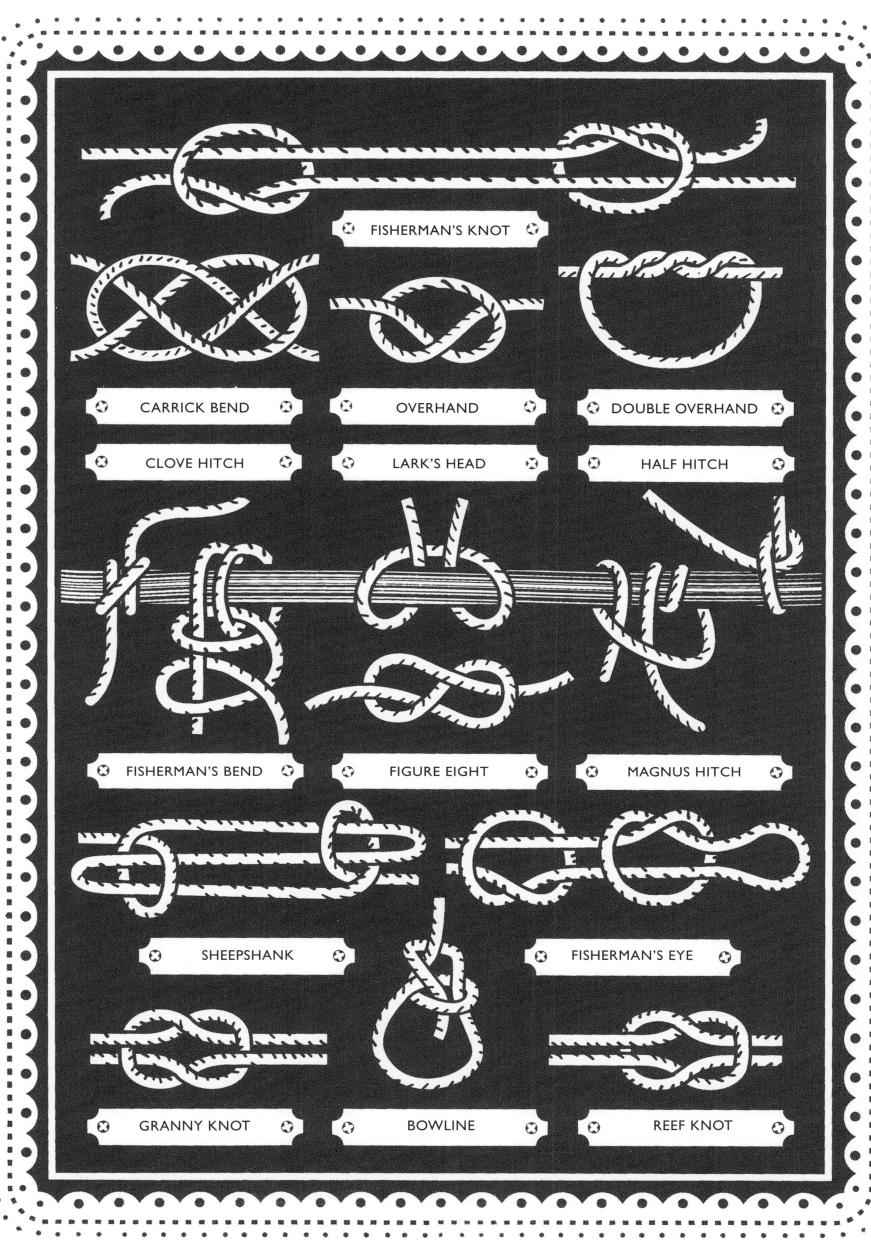

FISHERMAN'S KNOT

CARRICK BEND

OVERHAND

DOUBLE OVERHAND

CLOVE HITCH

LARK'S HEAD

HALF HITCH

FISHERMAN'S BEND

FIGURE EIGHT

MAGNUS HITCH

SHEEPSHANK

FISHERMAN'S EYE

GRANNY KNOT

BOWLINE

REEF KNOT

CLOUD CLASSIFICATION

Fluffy and white or gray and threatening, clouds can be forces of creation or destruction. They irrigate our crops — but they also bring ferocious storms. And though scientists have studied clouds intensively, we still don't fully understand how they work.

You don't have to be a genius to notice that no two clouds are exactly alike. But when British chemist Luke Howard named the clouds two hundred years ago, he was doing something extraordinary and new. He sorted them into three basic types: cirrus, cumulus, and stratus. He then introduced four categories for clouds that fit more than one of these types: cirrocumulus, cirrostratus, cumulostratus, and nimbus.

Howard's paper helped to establish meteorology (the study of weather and climate) on a scientific basis. His *Seven Lectures on Meteorology* (1837) was the first textbook on the subject.

FAME AND CONTROVERSY

His work made him famous, but Howard had several angry critics. They were furious that he gave the clouds Latin names. Today, we take this for granted. But if Howard's rivals had had their way, we would be calling clouds "flocks," "tufts," "piles," and "feathered arcs," or "stacken," "sonder," "wain," and "twain"!

VAST AND POWERFUL

Clouds are huge and heavy, and they hold extraordinary amounts of energy. A tropical cumulonimbus stores some 167 million kilowatt hours: enough to keep the lights on in New York City for nearly a day. The same cloud may be more than 11 miles high—twice the height of the world's tallest mountain—and weigh one million tons.

So how is it that they float, apparently weightless, above our heads? A cloud forms when warm air rises from the ground, carrying water vapor upward. It turns into droplets, releasing heat, which makes the cloud rise faster than before.

Other questions aren't as easy to answer. We aren't sure why clouds rise as fast as they do, or what controls their size; we don't really know what goes on inside them; and for fifty years, there were four different theories of how they turn to rain. The chief theory, called "tangling clustering instability," was proposed only in 2013. Two centuries after a modest chemist named the clouds, we have a lot left to learn about them.

HIPPIE HEAVEN

The phrase "on cloud nine" suggests blissful euphoria. Where did it come from? Nobody really knows, but the most common explanation given is that nine was the highest number in Luke Howard's scheme. But this is obviously false — Howard had only seven categories!

GOTCHA

Howard's work gained him many fans, among them the great German writer Johann Goethe. Goethe was so famous that when Howard first received a letter from him, he thought it was a friend playing a prank. Goethe went on to write poems about clouds in Howard's honor.

ELEPHANT CLOUDS

In Hindu and Buddhist mythology, clouds are the wandering spirits of elephant gods. The name for the Hindu god Airavata means "elephant of the clouds," and he is always shown as perfectly white in color, like a cumulus cloud.

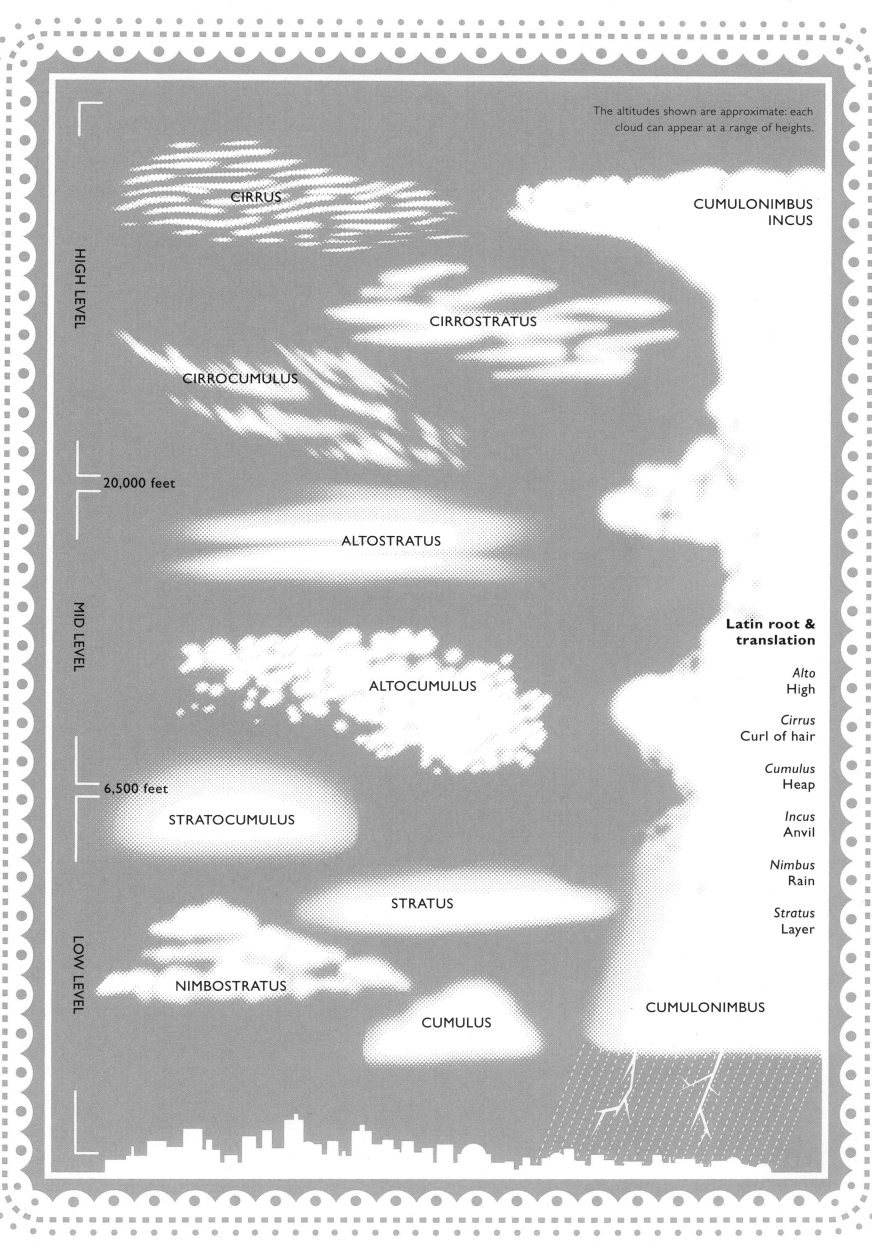

The altitudes shown are approximate: each cloud can appear at a range of heights.

CIRRUS

CUMULONIMBUS INCUS

HIGH LEVEL

CIRROSTRATUS

CIRROCUMULUS

20,000 feet

ALTOSTRATUS

MID LEVEL

Latin root & translation

Alto
High

ALTOCUMULUS

Cirrus
Curl of hair

Cumulus
Heap

6,500 feet

Incus
Anvil

STRATOCUMULUS

Nimbus
Rain

STRATUS

Stratus
Layer

LOW LEVEL

NIMBOSTRATUS

CUMULONIMBUS

CUMULUS

THE SOLAR SYSTEM

Before Nicolaus Copernicus put forward his theory in 1543, most people believed that the sun, stars, and planets were fixed inside a series of crystal spheres, all spinning around the earth.

This central-Earth theory was popular because it successfully predicted the movements of the heavens — and because it agreed with Bible teaching. So when Copernicus argued that Earth and the other planets circled the sun, he was mostly ignored. People only really started to pay attention when Italian astronomer Galileo Galilei used one of the first telescopes to prove Copernicus right in 1610.

PLANET OF THE DAY

The names for some of our days of the week come from objects in the solar system: Moon-day and Sun-day are obvious. The names of other days come from the Norse gods Tyr, Odin, Thor, and Frigg. Saturn-day comes from a Roman god.

DEMOTED PLANET

Seventy-six years after its discovery in 1930, Pluto, the outermost astronomical object shown here, got downgraded to a "dwarf planet." Why the change? Because other, bigger objects also orbiting the sun don't count as planets.

DISTANT AND IGNORED

With a telescope, Galileo was able to confirm six planets besides Earth. The most distant planets we have identified in our solar system are roughly twenty, thirty, and forty times farther from the sun than the earth is. To get a clearer sense of these distances, imagine that New York City is the sun and the earth is Washington, D.C.: Pluto would be in New Zealand.

IN SEARCH OF MARTIANS

Is there a chance that there might be life on another planet? Some can be ruled out immediately: the outer planets, for example, are too cold to support life. Saturn and Jupiter are made of gas and lack a solid surface. Mercury, the closest to the sun, has noon temperatures that could melt some metals.

Cloud-covered Venus once seemed a likely candidate: in 1903, Swedish scientist Svante Arrhenius imagined it as "dripping wet" and "covered by swamps." But when spacecraft flew under the clouds, they found dry, searing heat and a CO_2 atmosphere.

That leaves Mars. Nineteenth-century astronomers spotted what looked like channels on the planet's surface and thought they were canals built by aliens. The channels turned out to be an optical illusion, but in 2015 space probes confirmed that parts of the planet are wet: liquid water is vital for carbon-based life like Earth's plants and animals.

So if there is life on Mars, what does it look like? You can forget little green men — sadly, martians are far more likely to be bacteria.

Speeding at 186,282 miles a second, light from the sun reaches Earth in eight minutes, but it will zoom on for another five hours before reaching Pluto.

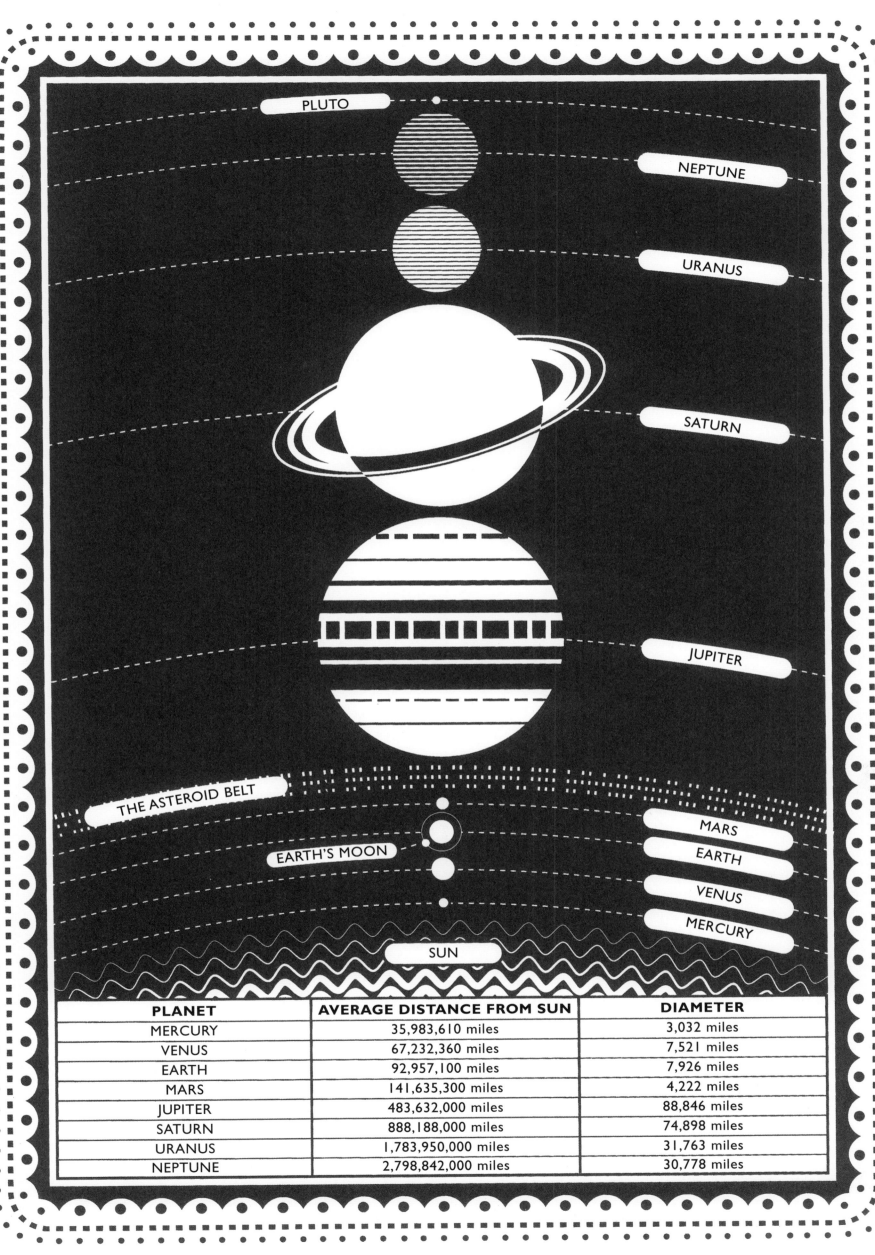

PLANET	AVERAGE DISTANCE FROM SUN	DIAMETER
MERCURY	35,983,610 miles	3,032 miles
VENUS	67,232,360 miles	7,521 miles
EARTH	92,957,100 miles	7,926 miles
MARS	141,635,300 miles	4,222 miles
JUPITER	483,632,000 miles	88,846 miles
SATURN	888,188,000 miles	74,898 miles
URANUS	1,783,950,000 miles	31,763 miles
NEPTUNE	2,798,842,000 miles	30,778 miles

ANATOMY
of TYPE

Modern typefaces are entirely digital, but most of their component parts would have been familiar to Johannes Gutenberg's punch cutters and typefounders in fifteenth-century Germany.

HAND MOLD

The parts of a hand mold snap together to fit any width of letter, from a broad W to a narrow i. A wooden cover stops the hot mold from burning the typefounder's hands.

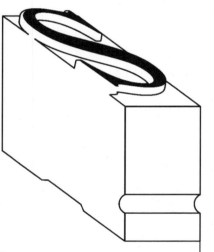

BEAUTIFUL TYPE

Though the Latin alphabet has only twenty-six letters, Gutenberg had his letter cutters create many more, because he wanted his books to be as beautiful as any hand-lettered manuscript. His 1454 Bible uses no fewer than 290 different characters.

PRINTED BIBLES

Gutenberg's big project was to print more than 200 Bibles. Most were on paper, but he also printed a deluxe edition on parchment made from the skin of 5,000 unborn calves.

Printing as we know it began in Mainz, Germany, in the workshop of goldsmith Johannes Gutenberg. He didn't invent printing from movable type (that happened in China) but he made it practical. His workers cast letters one by one from melted lead. They lined them up in a wooden press, dabbed ink on top, and carefully stamped them against damp paper to print pages.

Gutenberg borrowed most of this technology. His press came from a vineyard, his paper from monastic scribes, and his ink from oil painters. Ironically, his really original idea is largely forgotten.

Gutenberg's innovation was a type mold. It looked like a wooden puzzle with interlocking parts. Melted lead poured in the top flowed down to fill letter-shaped grooves in a brass plate placed underneath, called a matrix. Using one of these, even an unskilled type caster could mold 1,500 letters a day.

MASTER ENGRAVERS

The truly skilled work lay in creating the matrix into which the liquid metal flowed. Its letter-shaped grooves were made by striking it with a punch: a perfect replica of the letter, carved from steel.

The craftsmen who cut these punches were Gutenberg's type designers. For them, the leg, eye, counter, serif, and bowl were not just names for parts of letters; they were tiny pieces of steel to be shaved or filed into shape. The punch cutters did this with extraordinary skill. With a stroke of a graver, they could narrow a serif by just 0.001 mm.

Today, type-design software has a precision of one-thousandth the height of a capital letter: for type the size you are reading, that's about 0.004 mm.

Alas, Gutenberg's invention didn't make him rich. His scheming partner, Johann Fust, demanded repayment of a loan. Gutenberg lost his press, his job, and his Bibles.

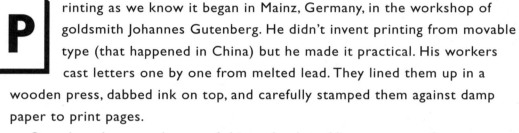

Gutenberg's type turned books from treasures for the super rich into affordable tools for spreading knowledge.

* * * * * * * * * * * * * * * * *

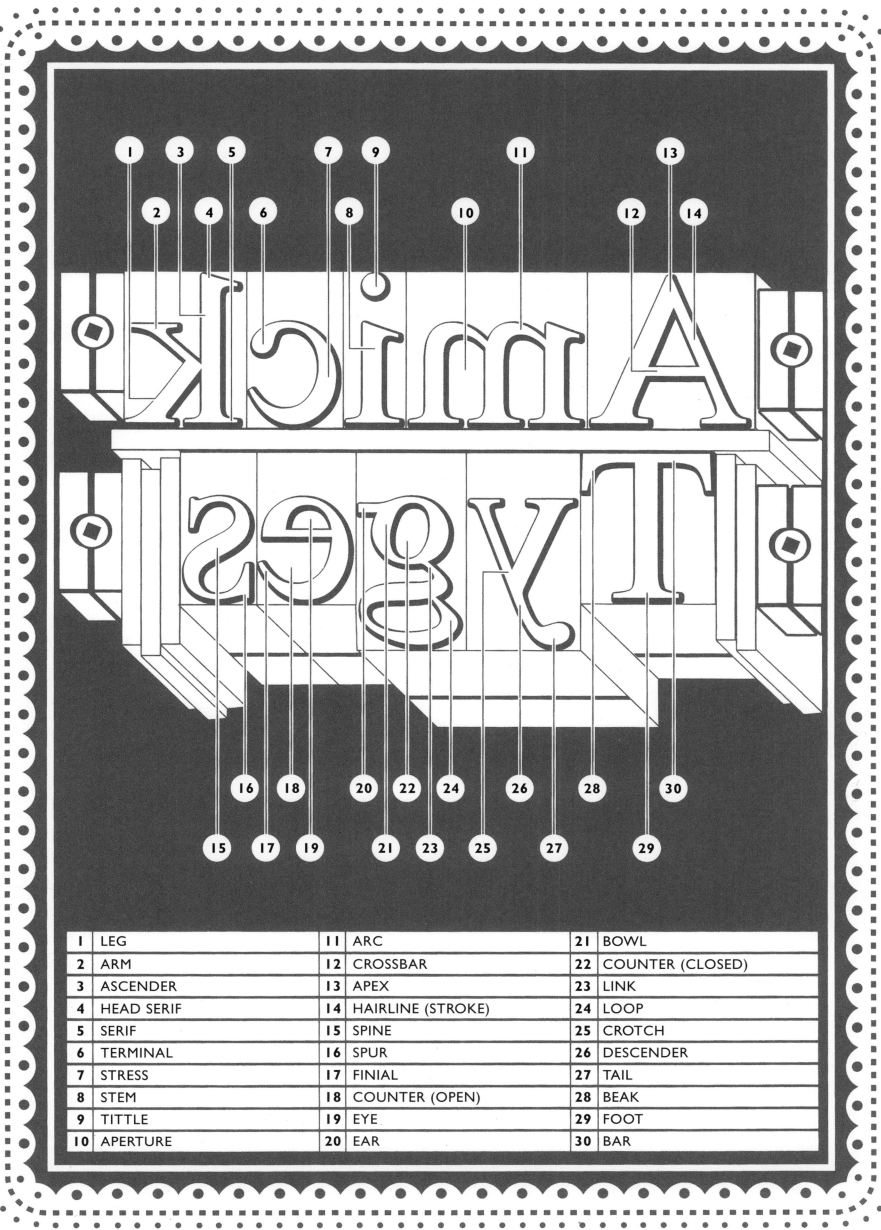

1	LEG	**11**	ARC	**21**	BOWL
2	ARM	**12**	CROSSBAR	**22**	COUNTER (CLOSED)
3	ASCENDER	**13**	APEX	**23**	LINK
4	HEAD SERIF	**14**	HAIRLINE (STROKE)	**24**	LOOP
5	SERIF	**15**	SPINE	**25**	CROTCH
6	TERMINAL	**16**	SPUR	**26**	DESCENDER
7	STRESS	**17**	FINIAL	**27**	TAIL
8	STEM	**18**	COUNTER (OPEN)	**28**	BEAK
9	TITTLE	**19**	EYE	**29**	FOOT
10	APERTURE	**20**	EAR	**30**	BAR

THE HUMAN
SKELETON

Our bones are miracles of natural engineering. They are made of immensely strong, rock-like material, yet their hollow structure makes them so light that champion athletes can jump higher than their heads.

Only when we break one of our 206 bones do we realize what an amazing job our skeleton normally does. It makes up just one-fifteenth of our body weight, yet it can withstand enormous pressure. For example, the bones in a child's arm are strong enough to support a car. And though our bones are rigid, our bodies bend—there's no itch we can't just about reach to scratch.

A SPARE FINGER
One in 200 of us has an extra rib or two, and about one in 500 has a sixth finger or toe.

Bones are a vital store for the body's minerals and energy.

These extraordinary capabilities come from the mineral that bone is made of: a calcium phosphate mineral known as apatite. Laid down exactly where it's needed as we grow, this material is an engineer's dream. Weight for weight, bone is ten times stronger than concrete.

BENDY BODIES

Our skeleton flexes and bends nimbly because it's made of lots and lots of individual bones, fixed together by a cunning arrangement of slipping, sliding, twisting, and folding joints. But just how many bones are there in a skeleton? It depends on how old you are and where you stop counting. Children have many more bones because as we grow up, our bones fuse together. For example, at the base of the spine, where a tail grew on our ape ancestors, four infant bones join up to form the adult coccyx.

If you counted the skeleton's teeniest bony bits, even a normal adult would have far more than 206. In the ear, tiny otolith bones, fine as dust, help us balance. In tendons and muscles, sesamoid "sesame-seed" bones grow in response to stress as we age. And in the pineal gland, deep in our brain, we grow tiny, gritty bone particles called "brain sand." Nobody knows why!

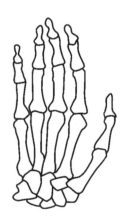

NOISY KNUCKLES
The CRACK! that your knuckles make when you bend them is the sound of the liquid between each of the bones boiling.

NOT SO FUNNY
Nobody really has a "funny bone." The tingling discomfort you get from a blow to the elbow is caused by pressure on a nerve.

DEM BONES, DEM DRY BONES!

When our lives end, our bones will be all that's left of us. A buried body decays within a few years, but the skeleton can survive for millennia. Dentists can identify a corpse from the teeth; forensic scientists can use a skeleton to judge age and sex; and from the size and shape of their bones, archaeologists can even guess what a person's occupation might have been when they were alive.

TASTY BONES
The fatty marrow inside our long bones is reportedly delicious when cooked. Archaeologists believe our ancestors were cannibals because they have found bones snapped open, seemingly intentionally, to get at the marrow within.

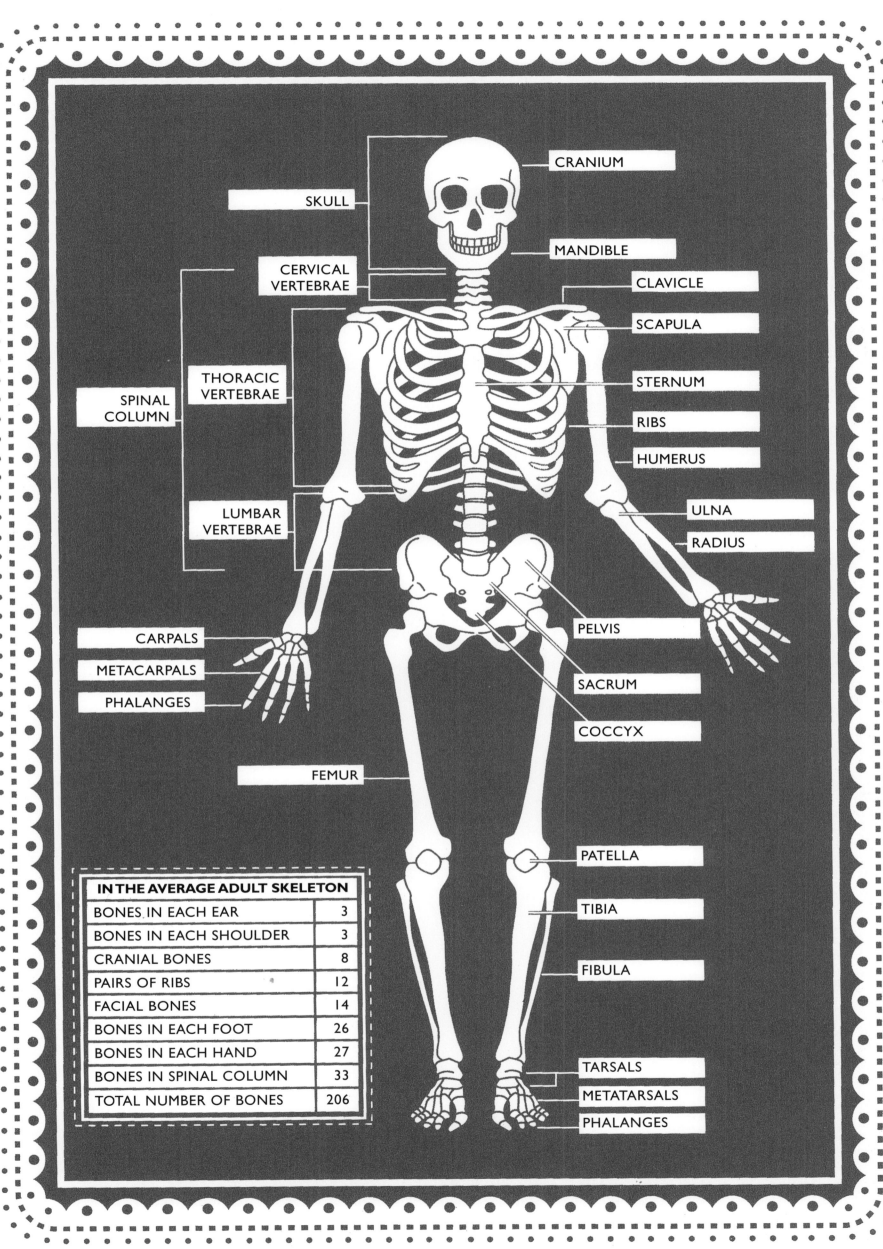

CRANIUM

SKULL

MANDIBLE

CERVICAL VERTEBRAE

CLAVICLE

SCAPULA

STERNUM

THORACIC VERTEBRAE

SPINAL COLUMN

RIBS

HUMERUS

ULNA

RADIUS

LUMBAR VERTEBRAE

CARPALS

METACARPALS

PHALANGES

PELVIS

SACRUM

COCCYX

FEMUR

PATELLA

TIBIA

FIBULA

TARSALS

METATARSALS

PHALANGES

IN THE AVERAGE ADULT SKELETON	
BONES IN EACH EAR	3
BONES IN EACH SHOULDER	3
CRANIAL BONES	8
PAIRS OF RIBS	12
FACIAL BONES	14
BONES IN EACH FOOT	26
BONES IN EACH HAND	27
BONES IN SPINAL COLUMN	33
TOTAL NUMBER OF BONES	206

SPELLING, MORSE, AND SEMAPHORE

ALPHABETS

Communication codes replace letters of the alphabet with flapping flags or the rapid dots and dashes of Morse code.

Sending a message has never been simpler than it is today, but there was a time when news traveled no faster on land than a messenger on a galloping horse. This changed in 1791, with the spread of the *télégraphe* ("far writer"): a network of French signaling towers. Flapping wooden arms on their roofs relayed coded messages between observers in adjacent towers.

With the turn of the century, navies adapted this system for use at sea, with handheld signal flags that represented the alphabet. Using the two-flag semaphore system shown here, sailors could sign up to seventeen words a minute. With large mechanical masthead flags and good weather, messages could travel 15 miles.

> *Flag semaphore remained an official way of sending a telegram until 1960.*

MORSE AND VAIL

Flag semaphore could only be used to communicate as far as the eye could see, and by the middle of the nineteenth century, several inventors had suggested sending messages down wires as pulses of electricity. The most successful system was pioneered by American painter and inventor Samuel Morse. His "electric telegraph" used short and long pulses ("dots and dashes") to stand for letters of the alphabet. Though it came to be called Morse code, it was developed by both Morse and his mechanic, Alfred Vail. To speed transmission, Vail gave common letters the shortest codes. He worked this out by visiting a printer and counting the letters in a case of lead type.

Morse established the first wires for his system in 1837. By 1861 telegraph cables crossed the American continent, and five years later an undersea cable linked the United States and Europe.

When the telephone was invented in 1876, telegraph wires began to carry voice calls, but telephone and later radio never quite killed off Morse code. It was used to send telegrams in the United States until 2006. Navies still use it with signal lights for flashing messages from ship to ship.

POW MORSE CODE
● ● ●　▬ ▬ ▬　● ● ●

When American soldier Jeremiah Denton was captured as a prisoner of war in North Vietnam in 1966, his captors put him on display in a TV broadcast. While he obediently answered questions, he opened and shut his eyes in a rhythm of long and short blinks. It was Morse code, and Denton was spelling out a secret message: "torture." It confirmed the suspicions of intelligence experts that he was being mistreated in Vietnamese custody.

HOTEL ECHO LIMA LIMA OSCAR!
Spelling alphabets such as the NATO code shown opposite replace letters with distinct words — helpful for noisy phone lines. The easily confused S and F become the unmistakable Sierra and Foxtrot. The Alpha-to-Zulu alphabet is used internationally, though some countries also have codes in their own languages.

MORSE COMEBACK
Fearing terrorists might use Morse code, some intelligence services, such as the Canadian Forces School of Electronics, are again teaching recruits to recognize, read, and send dot-and-dash signals.

ALPHA · -
BRAVO - · · ·
CHARLIE - · - ·
DELTA - · ·
ECHO ·
FOXTROT · · - ·

GOLF - - ·
HOTEL · · · ·
INDIA · ·
JULIET · - - -
KILO - · -
LIMA · - · ·

MIKE - -
NOVEMBER - ·
OSCAR - - -
PAPA · - - ·
QUEBEC - - · -
ROMEO · - ·

SIERRA · · ·
TANGO -
UNIFORM · · -
VICTOR · · · -
WHISKEY · - -
X-RAY - · · -

YANKEE - · - -
ZULU - - · ·
ZERO - - - - -
WUN · - - - -
TOO · · - - -
TREE · · · - -

FOWER · · · · -
FIFE · · · · ·
SIX - · · · ·
SEVEN - - · · ·
AIT - - - · ·
NINER - - - - ·

SIGNAL TO USE BEFORE NUMERALS. TO REVERT, USE "J."

ATOMIC
STRUCTURE

The idea that everything in our world is made from tiny little pieces is an ancient one, but evidence to support it only began to appear two hundred years ago. And the more we learn about atoms, the stranger they seem.

Ancient philosophers in Greece and India discussed the nature of our world from as early as the fifth century BCE. They guessed it was made of minute particles — but they could not prove it.

Atoms remained theoretical for 2,300 years, until English chemist John Dalton studied how oxygen and tin combine. They do so in two ways — one of which uses exactly twice as much oxygen as the other. Dalton suggested this could happen only if elements existed as separate, individual particles. Tin (Sn) reacts with either one or two oxygen atoms, to form stannous oxide (SnO) and tin dioxide (SnO_2).

ELECTRON BEAM

The first hint that atoms were made of still smaller particles came in 1897, when English physicist Sir J. J. Thomson showed that "rays" shining from a hot wire in a vacuum tube were actually beams of particles. Each particle was 1,800 times lighter than the lightest atom, hydrogen. Thomson had discovered electrons: negatively charged subparticles that spin around inside the atom.

But just *what* do they orbit? This was discovered twelve years later when scientists fired a stream of particles at gold foil. They wanted to test the accepted "plum pudding" theory of atomic structure, in which the negative electron "plums" were evenly distributed in a positively charged cloud (the "pudding"). Had this been accurate, the particles would have passed straight through; but a few bounced off. This could happen only if each gold atom had a nucleus (center) of positively charged particles — protons — with a crowd of electrons around it.

The word atom comes from the Greek atomos, which means "indivisible."

TRULY TINY
The iron atom pictured opposite is about 150 picometers across: 7 million of them lined up in a row would span 1 mm.

Fe 26 / IRON 56

SCHRÖDINGER'S CAT
The fact that particles don't have properties until we measure them worried Austrian physicist Erwin Schrödinger. In 1935 he imagined a cat sealed in a box with a glass tube containing poison gas, some radioactive particles, and a sensor. The sensor, on detecting the decay of a radioactive particle, breaks the glass tube, thus releasing the poison gas. Schrödinger suggested that until we open the box, the cat may be considered both alive and dead.

SECRETS OF THE ATOM

Researchers quickly learned more.

Studies in 1913 revealed that electrons orbit in shells at fixed distances from the nucleus, and in 1932 it was found that, as well as protons, the nucleus contains particles with no charge, called neutrons.

The atom had given up its secrets, but its tiny world was stranger than anyone could have possibly dreamed. On such a small scale, the rules that govern our own world don't apply. We now know that particles have properties, such as spin direction, only when we measure them: until then, we can only guess at what they might be doing.

ATOMIC NUMBER	26	
CHEMICAL SYMBOL	Fe	
CHEMICAL NAME	IRON	
MASS NUMBER	56	

Fe 26 / IRON 56

PROTON	+	POSITIVE ELECTRICAL CHARGE
NEUTRON	●	NO ELECTRICAL CHARGE
ELECTRON	–	NEGATIVE ELECTRICAL CHARGE

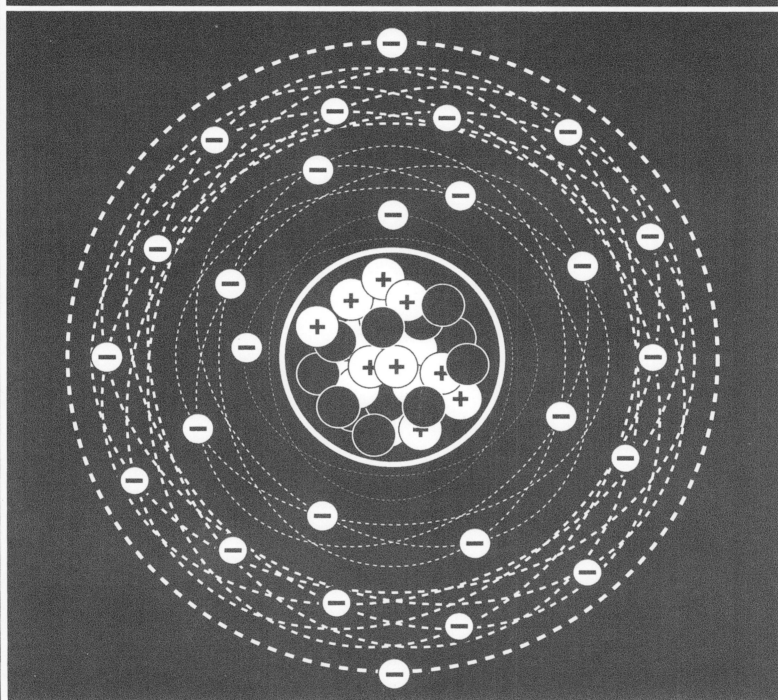

THE IRON ATOM SHOWN HERE IS THAT OF THE COMMONEST IRON ISOTOPE, ^{56}Fe; OTHER ISOTOPES EXIST WITH THE SAME NUMBER AND ARRANGEMENT OF PROTONS AND ELECTRONS, BUT WITH DIFFERENT NUMBERS OF NEUTRONS.

ELECTRON CONFIGURATION

SHELL		QUANTITY
1 (K)		2
2 (L)		8
3 (M)		14
4 (N)		2
		TOTAL –26

NUCLEUS

SUBATOMIC PARTICLE	QUANTITY
PROTON	26
NEUTRON	30

THE GOLDEN RATIO
&
THE FIBONACCI SEQUENCE

What's the secret of beauty? According to some of the world's most respected thinkers, it's a ratio. The golden ratio has set the proportions of countless works of art and occurs with fascinating regularity in the natural world.

Φ

DESPITE THE APPEAL OF THE GOLDEN RATIO, THERE IS NO SOLID PROOF THAT IT'S MORE PLEASING TO THE EYE THAN ANY OTHER PROPORTION.

Ever since the architects of ancient Egypt planned their magnificent pyramids, musicians, artists, and mathematicians have tried to achieve perfect balance and beauty in their work. In the fourth century BCE, the Greek mathematician Euclid gave the first known definition of the golden ratio (also called the golden section or the golden mean). This is the splitting of a line or shape into unequal parts so that, as Euclid wrote, "as the whole line is to the greater segment, so is the greater to the lesser," which is widely believed to be an elegant and visually satisfying design.

BEAUTIFUL FIGURES
Renaissance genius Leonardo da Vinci illustrated a 1509 book about the golden ratio and also used it in his work. Hundreds of years later, artists such as Georges Seurat and Salvador Dalí used the ratio in their paintings and sculptures.

FINDING GOLD
People who believe in the golden ratio look hard for examples of it — and always find them. One person measured the height of 65 women, and that of their navels, and reported that their ratio was the same every time.

MICROSCOPIC SPIRALS
When Chinese scientists chilled bubbles of silica, each one-hundredth of a millimeter across, spiraling rows of bumps formed on their surfaces in patterns that followed the Fibonacci sequence (see opposite page).

SERIOUS SERIES

Italian mathematician Leonardo Fibonacci calculated the golden ratio eight hundred years ago with a series of numbers that still bears his name. Beginning with the number 1, he added another 1 to get 2. Then he added each number to the one before, like this:

1, 1, 2, 3, 5, 8, 13, 21, 34 . . .

Dividing any of these numbers by the one before it (with the exception of 1, 2, and 3) calculates the golden ratio (1.61803398875 . . .). What's amazing is that the series doesn't have to start with 1 and 1 — you can use any two digits.

The golden ratio is such a significant number that in 1909 American mathematician Mark Barr gave it the Greek letter phi (Φ). He chose phi because it's the first letter of Phidias, which was the name of a fifth-century-BCE Greek architect who used the ratio in his work.

THE NUMBER IN NATURE

Even nature obeys this extraordinary law. The same pattern defines the gracefully curling shape of a nautilus shell and the spiraling spikes of a pineapple. Of course, nature knows nothing of mathematics. The ratio occurs because it provides the most efficient spacing for growth. Leaves sprouting from a stem at angles defined by the Fibonacci sequence grow to capture the most sunlight possible, with the least shading of the leaves below.

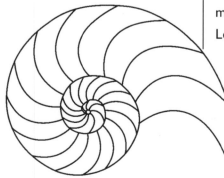

Phi has some unique properties as a number. Adding 1 to it produces the square of phi (Φ x Φ). And subtracting 1 gives its reciprocal (1/Φ).

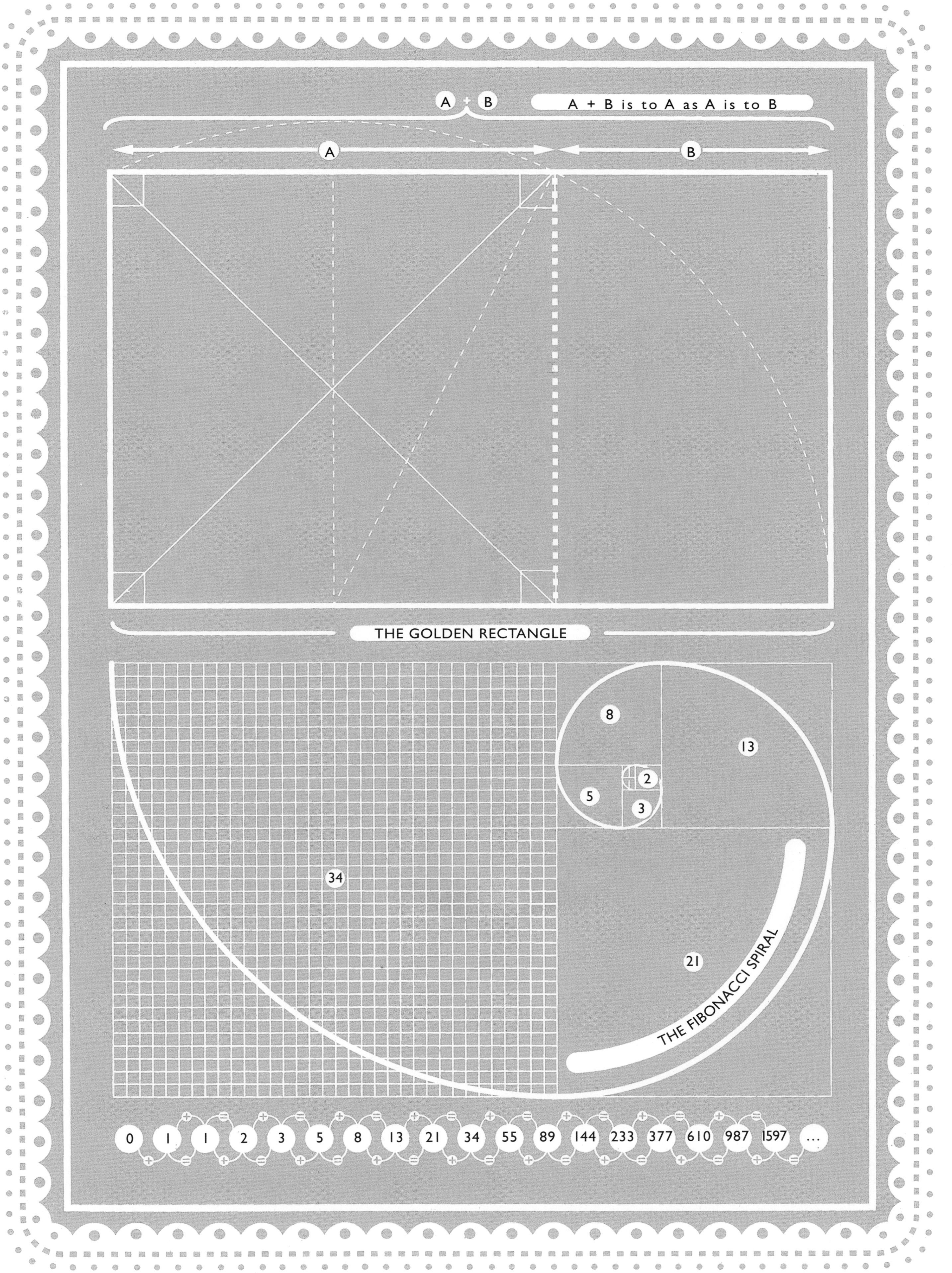

A + B

A + B is to A as A is to B

A

B

THE GOLDEN RECTANGLE

8

13

2

5

3

34

21

THE FIBONACCI SPIRAL

0　1　1　2　3　5　8　13　21　34　55　89　144　233　377　610　987　1597　...

MUSIC NOTATION

Since people first began to sing, musicians have passed on themes, riffs, and whole songs by listening to one another. But to make music last longer than an echo, they had to figure out a way of writing it down.

We don't know who was the first to put music to paper, but by the fourth century BCE, Greek musicians had begun using letters of their alphabet to show the rising and falling pattern of a tune. To signify a slightly higher (sharp) or lower (flat) pitch of a note, they turned letters sideways or upside down. The Greek system grew until, by the fourth century CE, it included more than 1,600 different musical symbols.

INTRODUCING NEUMES

By the ninth century, a new notation had begun to emerge. Monks singing in Christian worship marked their song sheets with *neumes*—from a Greek word for "sign" or "breath." These tick marks reminded them how the pitch changed from note to note but gave little real indication of which note to sing.

Then, in the tenth century, an anonymous music copyist ruled a straight red line above the words of a song to represent the F note below middle C. The position of the neumes above and below the line showed their pitch. The line was called a staff, or stave, from an old German word meaning "firm" or "fixed."

This worked so well that a second line was added above, and then a third. The following century, Italian monk Guido d'Arezzo (see right) suggested using four or five lines, creating the stave familiar to today's musicians.

DIG THAT CRAZY RHYTHM

Of course, music isn't just about pitch: rhythm is just as important. At first, neumes could not properly reflect this, but they gradually evolved. By the thirteenth century, the monks copying plainchant music were no longer using sloping lines but instead drew neat squares on or between the lines. It was a short step to using these marks' shape to indicate the length of the notes. Within a century, music copyists had turned the square into a diamond to represent a half note. To show a long note, they attached a little tail, so that the note resembled a small flag. By the fifteenth century, the system of black notes on five lines that we use today was virtually complete.

DO-RE-MI MAN

Guido d'Arezzo not only perfected modern notation but also invented the do-re-mi scale of rising notes that helps budding musicians learn their scales. D'Arezzo realized that each of the lines of a famous hymn to John the Baptist began one note higher than the line before. The lines began with the syllables "Ut-re-mi-fa-sol-la." Ut was later changed to do because it was easier to sing.

Guido d'Arezzo's improvements to notation cut the time required to teach monks music from ten years to two.

WHAT, NO MUSIC?

Outside Europe, detailed notation has not always been important. In Japan, for example, much musical knowledge was passed down by ear, and musicians' guilds guarded their tunes jealously. The surviving notation only hints at how these "secret" pieces were performed.

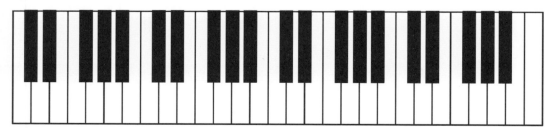

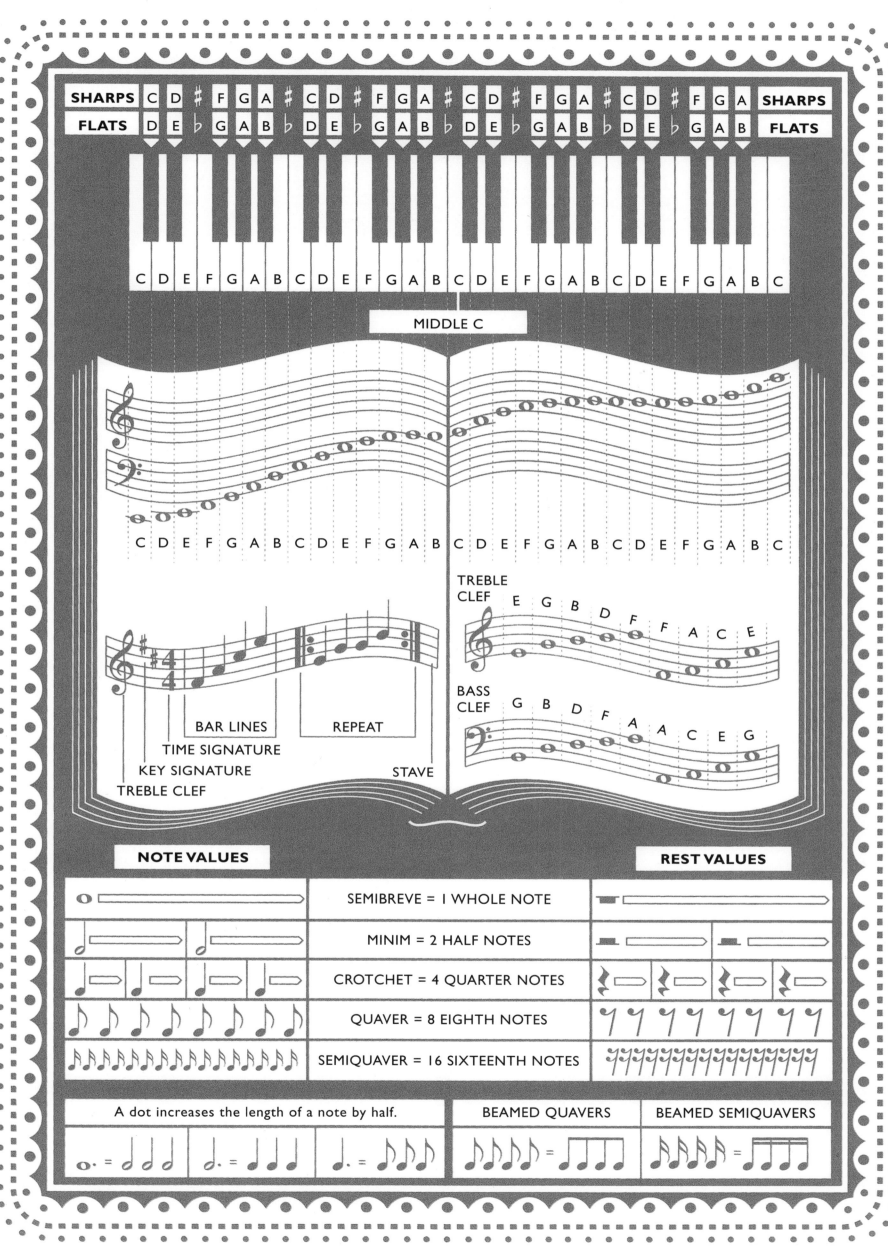

THE ANATOMY OF A BICYCLE

When it was perfected at the end of the nineteenth century, the humble bicycle transformed transportation— and helped launch the very first women's movement.

RACY RACERS
Laufmaschines also appeared on stage: scantily clad acrobats rode them to entertain audiences at music halls.

UNDERCOVER CYCLISTS
American women caused a sensation when they first cycled in "bifurcated nether garments" (trousers). Newspapers reported in 1894 that more than one hundred women were cycling in New York — but only at night, when nobody could see them.

SHEEPSHEARING
Bicycle technology made sheepshearing easier: around 1900, several companies introduced bike-powered fleece clippers. Propped up on a stand and pedaled by a boy, a bicycle could power clippers for two shearers.

Two-wheeled travel began in 1817 when German forestry official Baron Karl von Drais set out to replace the horse. He gave his wooden running machine, or *Laufmaschine*, two wheels, and handlebars for steering, but it lacked pedals—riders had to kick themselves along.

Bicycles developed in strange and dangerous ways. By 1870 an "ordinary" bicycle had a huge wheel at the front and a tiny one behind. The saddle was as high as a man's shoulder, and a fall from one of these machines could be dangerous. In Britain they were nicknamed "penny-farthings," with the rear wheel represented by the smallest coin, the farthing, and the front wheel represented by the much bigger penny, which was worth four times as much.

SAFE, MODERN BICYCLES

Then, in 1885, English inventor John Starley produced a bicycle with a radically better design. His Rover cycle had a diamond-shaped frame, similar-sized wheels, a chain drive with pedals, and handlebars connected directly to the front forks. In most ways, it resembled the modern bicycle shown opposite.

These "safety" bicycles were not cheap, costing nine weeks' wages for a factory worker, but they could be found for less secondhand and were not nearly as expensive as horses, which required a stable and feed. On a bicycle, people too poor to own a horse could travel farther and more quickly in a day than they could walk.

FREEWHEELING WORLD

For women, the bicycle was—literally—liberating. In 1896, American feminist Susan B. Anthony said that "bicycling . . . has done more to emancipate women than anything else in the world. . . . I stand and rejoice every time I see a woman ride by on a wheel . . . the picture of free, untrammeled womanhood." The bicycle gave women the freedom to travel and relieved them of corsets and ankle-length dresses. Instead they wore "rational dress"—baggy trousers called knickerbockers. These "New Women" wanted more than just the right to cycle. Before long, they demanded, and won, something much more important: the right to vote.

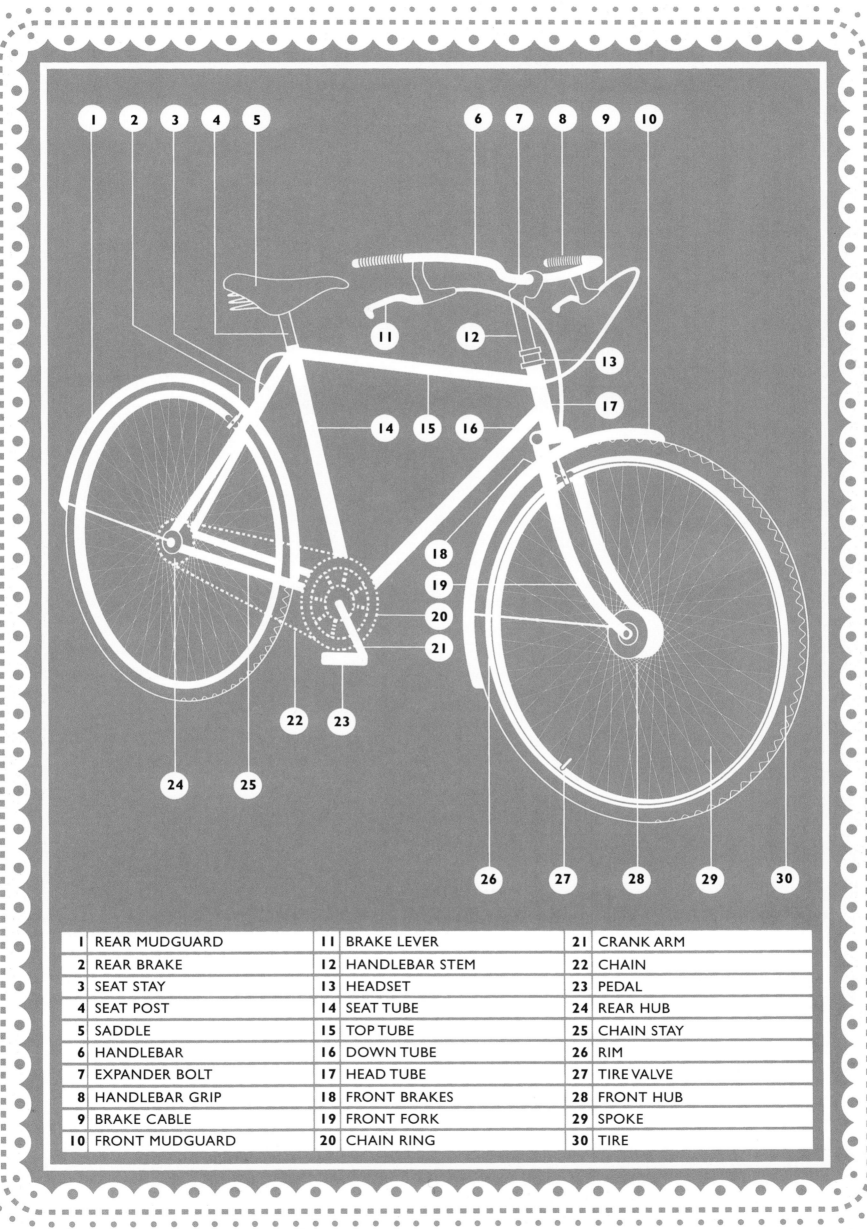

1	REAR MUDGUARD	11	BRAKE LEVER	21	CRANK ARM
2	REAR BRAKE	12	HANDLEBAR STEM	22	CHAIN
3	SEAT STAY	13	HEADSET	23	PEDAL
4	SEAT POST	14	SEAT TUBE	24	REAR HUB
5	SADDLE	15	TOP TUBE	25	CHAIN STAY
6	HANDLEBAR	16	DOWN TUBE	26	RIM
7	EXPANDER BOLT	17	HEAD TUBE	27	TIRE VALVE
8	HANDLEBAR GRIP	18	FRONT BRAKES	28	FRONT HUB
9	BRAKE CABLE	19	FRONT FORK	29	SPOKE
10	FRONT MUDGUARD	20	CHAIN RING	30	TIRE

THE STRUCTURE & ATMOSPHERE of PLANET EARTH

Human beings may be the dominant species on Earth, but our success is confined to the planet's surface. We have hardly explored beneath our world's crust, and gravity and thin air make it difficult to soar very far above it.

Until about four hundred years ago, the suggestion that the earth was solid seemed absurd. The existence of caves suggested a hollow world — perhaps a hell — underground. It was an idea that proved hard to shake off. As late as 1818, American army officer John Symmes suggested that the earth was "hollow, habitable within, and widely open about the poles."

Geologists have since learned a lot more about Earth's structure, though most of their evidence remains indirect. The world's deepest mine drills just 2.5 miles into the earth's crust, so how do we know what's lower down?

The best clue that the earth is not hollow is gravity. Gravity gives everything its weight, and it's proportional to the planet's mass. If the earth were hollow, we would weigh less. Magma spewing from volcanoes shows there's liquid rock down there, but Earth's magnetic field tells us that it's not all liquid. There must be a solid iron core, like a giant magnet. Earthquakes tell us more: by timing their shock waves, geologists learned that the earth's core floats in a liquid outer core, enclosed by a stickier mantle.

FLIGHT ADVANTAGES

A few birds fly into the stratosphere: bar-headed geese can fly over Everest, the world's highest peak, at 30,000 feet. Aircraft also fly into the stratosphere to avoid the turbulence caused by storms and clouds. This high up, there is too little oxygen to support human life, so the air in the fuselage is compressed to the same density as the atmosphere 6,500 feet above sea level.

The summit of the earth's highest mountain, Everest, reaches the top of the breathable atmosphere.

ABOVE OUR HEADS

The earth's atmosphere is easier to observe, if no simpler to explore. Human beings live in the bottom 18,000 feet, where there is enough oxygen to survive. This habitable layer is about half of the *troposphere,* where almost all water vapor is located. The warmer *stratosphere* is heated by the sun's rays, preventing clouds from rising above it.

The cooler layers immediately beyond the stratosphere are collectively called the *ionosphere,* because their gases are partly ionized. Energy from the sun knocks electrons off them, leaving them with a positive electrical charge. This charge makes the ionosphere reflect radio waves, and this is how broadcasts bend around the earth's surface instead of beaming straight out into space.

Above the ionosphere, Earth's atmosphere turns to plasma, a mix of electrons and positively charged particles. This layer protects us from the solar wind — charged particles from the sun, heated to one million degrees Celsius. Without it, the solar wind would strip our atmosphere of oxygen.

SPACE

THE EXOSPHERE 621 MILES

THE THERMOSPHERE 53–621 MILES

THE MESOSPHERE 31–53 MILES

THE STRATOSPHERE 9–31 MILES

THE OZONE LAYER

THE TROPOSPHERE 0–9 MILES

CRUST

UPPER MANTLE

LOWER MANTLE

OUTER CORE

INNER CORE

0
37
410
SOLID
1,802
LIQUID
3,169
SOLID

3,958 MILES

GREEK ALPHABET

There were ways of writing before the Greek alphabet, but none that recorded vowel sounds. Our Latin alphabet grew out of the twenty-four Greek letters, and we still use the original letters in mathematics.

O ne of the very first things children are taught in school is a pair of Greek letters. The word "alphabet" comes from the first two Greek characters: *alpha,* written α, and *beta,* β. And when they learn the letters of the English language, children are studying an alphabet that was copied from Greek.

Greek wasn't the first written language. That was probably Sumerian, which was used in what is now Iraq. It didn't have letters but instead represented objects and ideas as "logograms"—tiny pictures. The first letters, which stood for the sounds of speech, weren't Greek, either. They came from Phoenicia, an empire that centered on what is now Lebanon, some 3,000 years ago.

BIG AND SMALL LETTERS

Greek capital letters have straight lines because they were scraped on pottery or carved in stone. Lowercase letters α to ω came into use in the ninth century CE, when people were using brushes or pens to write at speed on animal skin or paper.

TURNING THE OX

Greek writing was generally from left to right, like most European languages—but for a while scribes wrote back and forth across the page, in particular for stone inscriptions. They called this way of writing boustrophedon, *meaning "ox-turning," after the way a bull plows a field.*

PHOENICIA TO GREECE

Greece was about nine days' sailing from Phoenicia, and Phoenician traders brought their written language to Greece in the eighth century BCE. Not only did the Greeks borrow their alphabet; they also took the names of the letters from the Phoenicians, who had called them after words that began with each one. For some letters, you can even see the shape of the logogram that turned into the letter—the sound sign. For instance, the Greek *kappa,* written κ, comes from the Phoenician letter name *kap,* which means "hand," and looks like outstretched fingers.

The Greeks adapted Phoenician letters to write the different sounds of their own speech. In particular, the Phoenicians had no vowels. For these, the Greeks repurposed spare Phoenician letters that represented throaty, gargling sounds not spoken in Greece.

GREEK TO LATIN

The Romans adopted the Greek alphabet around the seventh century BCE. They turned it into the Latin letters that we now use to write in all western European languages.

Scientists still use Greek letters widely as names for variables (numbers that change) and fixed values. Best known is *pi,* π, the ratio of the outside of a circle to its diameter. We also use the first few letters like numbers: the "alpha male" in a group is the most powerful (first) man, and beta software is the test (second) version before a program is released to the public.

American college clubs started taking their names from Greek letters in 1775.

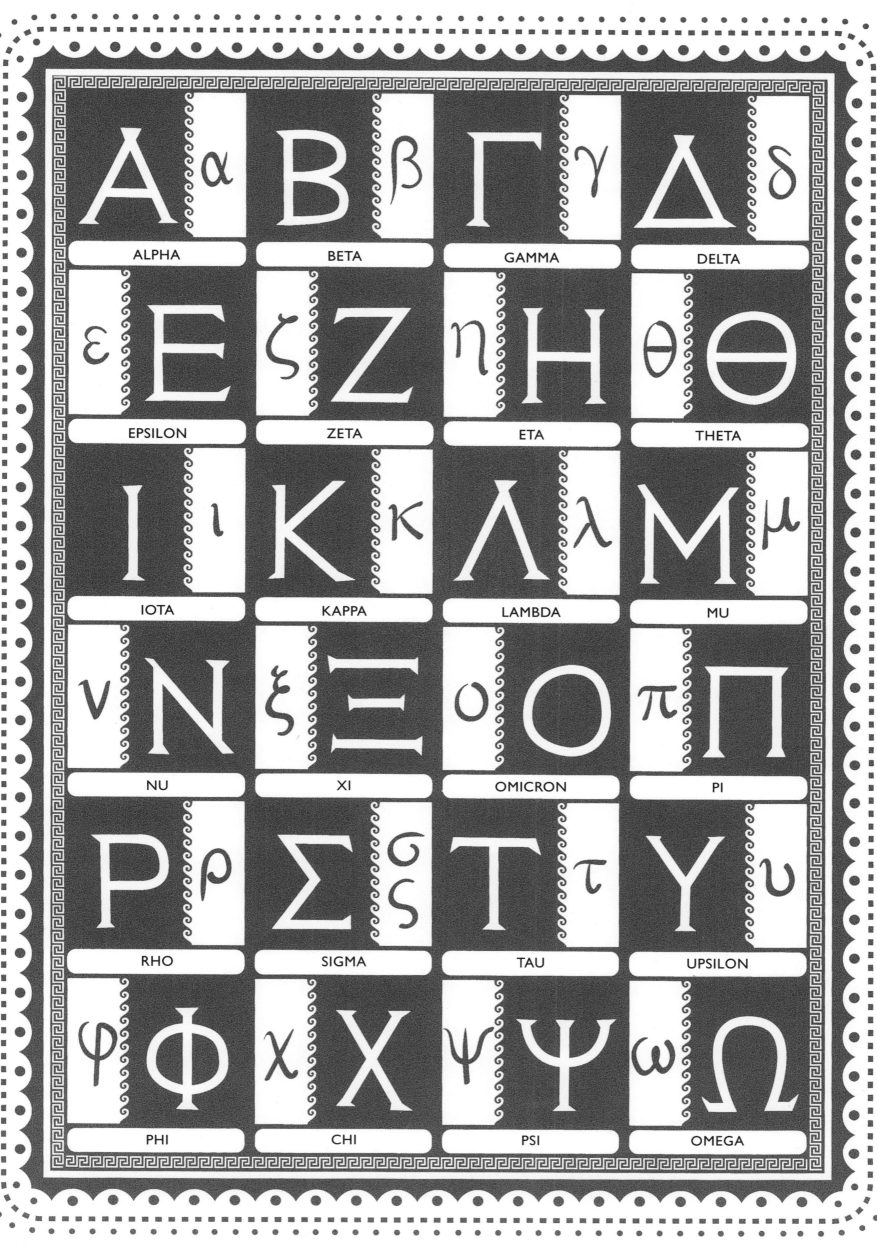

A α **ALPHA**	B β **BETA**	Γ γ **GAMMA**	Δ δ **DELTA**
E ε **EPSILON**	Z ζ **ZETA**	H η **ETA**	Θ θ **THETA**
I ι **IOTA**	K κ **KAPPA**	Λ λ **LAMBDA**	M μ **MU**
N ν **NU**	Ξ ξ **XI**	O ο **OMICRON**	Π π **PI**
P ρ **RHO**	Σ σ **SIGMA**	T τ **TAU**	Y υ **UPSILON**
Φ φ **PHI**	X χ **CHI**	Ψ ψ **PSI**	Ω ω **OMEGA**

SCREWS & NAILS

Screws and nails revolutionized construction, making it simple to join timbers together without skillfully sawed joints. Their evolution spans 9,000 years of history.

The very first nails were not made of metal at all. Stone-age craftsmen carefully shaved oak heartwood into "treenails" (number 2 on the opposite page) and hammered them into pre-drilled holes to keep joints together.

For much of their history, nails were precious. They were made entirely by hand from copper, bronze, and later iron. All metals were scarce and hard to extract. Carpenters who could afford them used nails carefully, often clinching them (bending over the ends) so that they would grip the wood as tightly as possible.

The scarceness of nails gave them a value far beyond their practical uses. In ancient Greece, iron nails were called *obols*; six of them made up a handful, or *drachma*. Used for payment, nails were replaced by silver coins only at the start of the seventh century BCE. "Drachma" remained the name of Greece's official currency until they adopted the euro in 2001.

THE TURNING OF THE SCREW

Screws came into use far later than nails, because their spiraling threads were extraordinarily difficult to make by hand. Italian engineer Agostino Ramelli drew them in his book *Various and Ingenious Machines* in 1588, but nearly two hundred years passed before screws became common. The first screw-making machines were patented in 1760, but they made parallel-sided screws (resembling number 20, opposite). Pointy wood screws like those we use today appeared a century or so later.

The heads of screws show a bewildering and extraordinary variety. The first were like bolt heads and turned with a wrench. Countersunk heads with slots were developed so that carpenters could hide hinges in the edges of doors: a raised screwhead stopped the door from closing.

SAILORS' GIFTS
Captain James Cook wrote in his diary that Pacific Islanders considered nails more welcome gifts than flowers. In 1767, according to popular legend, the crew of one ship, the HMS Dolphin, pulled so many nails from it as gifts for their sweethearts that the ship was in danger of coming apart.

COFFIN KEEPER
"One-way" screws, which cannot be unscrewed, were patented in 1796 as coffin fasteners. They aimed to foil grave robbers, who dug up corpses to sell to medical students studying anatomy.

NAIL LAWS
Nails were so valuable in colonial America that people burned down houses when they abandoned them to recover the nails. This was very wasteful, and the Virginia government eventually outlawed the fires to save the houses. Officials estimated the weight of the nails used in construction, and the state paid their value to the house owner as compensation instead.

SLIPPERY SLOTS

Other shapes work better than slots. Screws with socket heads stay on the screwdriver, leaving the worker's other hand free. Cross-head screws, invented in the 1930s, are easier to locate with the tip of the screwdriver, though they slip off if you turn too hard. This is a source of frustration for carpenters, but the screws were designed in this way to prevent the head from being damaged by ham-fisted artisans.

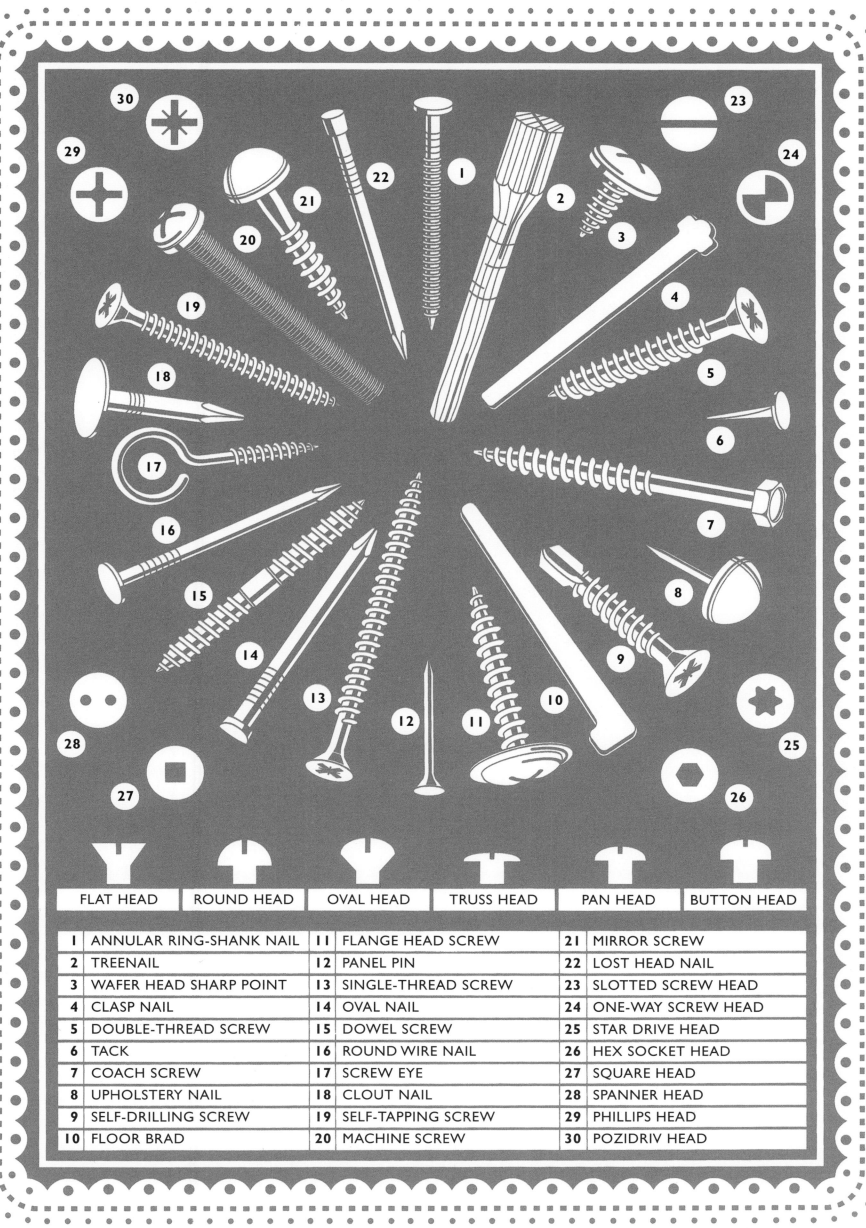

FLAT HEAD	ROUND HEAD	OVAL HEAD	TRUSS HEAD	PAN HEAD	BUTTON HEAD

1	ANNULAR RING-SHANK NAIL	11	FLANGE HEAD SCREW	21	MIRROR SCREW
2	TREENAIL	12	PANEL PIN	22	LOST HEAD NAIL
3	WAFER HEAD SHARP POINT	13	SINGLE-THREAD SCREW	23	SLOTTED SCREW HEAD
4	CLASP NAIL	14	OVAL NAIL	24	ONE-WAY SCREW HEAD
5	DOUBLE-THREAD SCREW	15	DOWEL SCREW	25	STAR DRIVE HEAD
6	TACK	16	ROUND WIRE NAIL	26	HEX SOCKET HEAD
7	COACH SCREW	17	SCREW EYE	27	SQUARE HEAD
8	UPHOLSTERY NAIL	18	CLOUT NAIL	28	SPANNER HEAD
9	SELF-DRILLING SCREW	19	SELF-TAPPING SCREW	29	PHILLIPS HEAD
10	FLOOR BRAD	20	MACHINE SCREW	30	POZIDRIV HEAD

IMPOSSIBLE
SHAPES

Teasing and tantalizing, these strange images appear to defy all logic. They intrigue us because each part makes perfect sense, yet the object as a whole is absurd.

An endless staircase, a bizarre disjointed triangle, and a puzzling fork. These illusions seem like simple parlor tricks, yet they have proven so compelling that researchers have written more than a hundred scientific papers on how they work and why our brains are fooled by them.

MASTER OF THE IMPOSSIBLE

Dutch artist Maurits Cornelis Escher is famous for his use of impossible objects. In the late 1950s and early '60s he made a series of hugely popular prints on this theme, including an endless staircase and a stream of water that apparently flows uphill.

WHO INVENTED THEM?

The original impossible shape was based on the triangle, and it had not one but two inventors. In 1934, as an eighteen-year-old schoolboy, Swedish artist Oscar Reutersvärd sketched his three-sided pattern of cubes. British mathematician Roger Penrose drew a similar triangle twenty-four years later, despite never having seen Reutersvärd's cubes. The publication of the Penrose triangle in a psychology journal helped to spread interest in impossible figures.

HOW DO THEY WORK?

Of the many impossible shapes, the Penrose triangle is one of the simplest to understand. At each corner, the triangle uses the ordinary conventions of perspective to imitate a 60-degree angle.

Cover up one corner with your thumb. Someone with simple craft skills could build the object you can now see. Next lift your thumb, and look at the corner it was covering. That is where the trickery lies: a line that should be at the front, if this were a real object, is drawn at the back. We fall for the lie because normally when we see a picture of overlapping objects, the one that's covered up is the one that's farther away.

The trick is more obvious in the impossible cube: the upright edge on the left at the back is drawn to pass over the horizontal edge at the front top.

We know that these objects cannot exist, yet our brains still try to make sense of them.

NOT SO IMPOSSIBLE

Though these objects seem impossible, it's actually not difficult to create a real Penrose triangle. However, there's a catch: the illusion works only from a single viewpoint. Turn the triangle or move your head and you'll realize immediately that only two of the corners join up.

REUTERSVÄRD TRIANGLE

BLIVET

MÖBIUS STRIP

IMPOSSIBLE CUBE

PENROSE TRIANGLE

PENROSE STAIRS

TIME ZONES
& TECTONIC PLATES

Mapping the world's tectonic plates and time zones creates a complicated jigsaw puzzle of drifting continents and hours lost or gained.

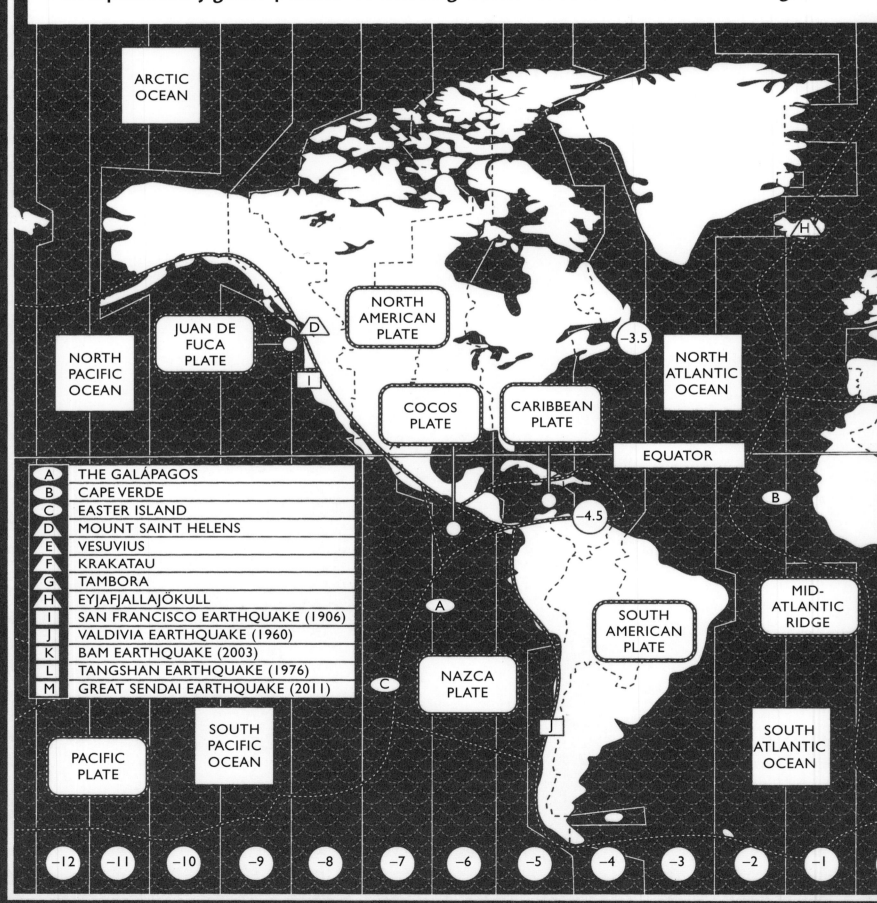

ARCTIC OCEAN

NORTH AMERICAN PLATE

JUAN DE FUCA PLATE

NORTH PACIFIC OCEAN

−3.5

NORTH ATLANTIC OCEAN

COCOS PLATE

CARIBBEAN PLATE

EQUATOR

B

−4.5

A | THE GALÁPAGOS
B | CAPE VERDE
C | EASTER ISLAND
D | MOUNT SAINT HELENS
E | VESUVIUS
F | KRAKATAU
G | TAMBORA
H | EYJAFJALLAJÖKULL
I | SAN FRANCISCO EARTHQUAKE (1906)
J | VALDIVIA EARTHQUAKE (1960)
K | BAM EARTHQUAKE (2003)
L | TANGSHAN EARTHQUAKE (1976)
M | GREAT SENDAI EARTHQUAKE (2011)

MID-ATLANTIC RIDGE

SOUTH AMERICAN PLATE

NAZCA PLATE

SOUTH PACIFIC OCEAN

SOUTH ATLANTIC OCEAN

PACIFIC PLATE

−12   −11   −10   −9   −8   −7   −6   −5   −4   −3   −2   −1

Our planet's map hasn't always looked like this. Though apparently fixed, the pattern of the continents changes constantly. Afloat on the earth's soft mantle (see pages 24–25), the tectonic plates that make up its crust move at the speed our hair and fingernails grow. Yet where they meet, their gentle journeys cause devastation as magma spills from volcanoes, or earthquakes release pent-up energy.

Continental drift has been happening slowly for three billion years, but time zones began only with the spread of railways in the nineteenth century. Before then, towns kept their own time, observing the sun's zenith. But speeding trains forced nations to synchronize clocks to avoid timetable clashes and train crashes.

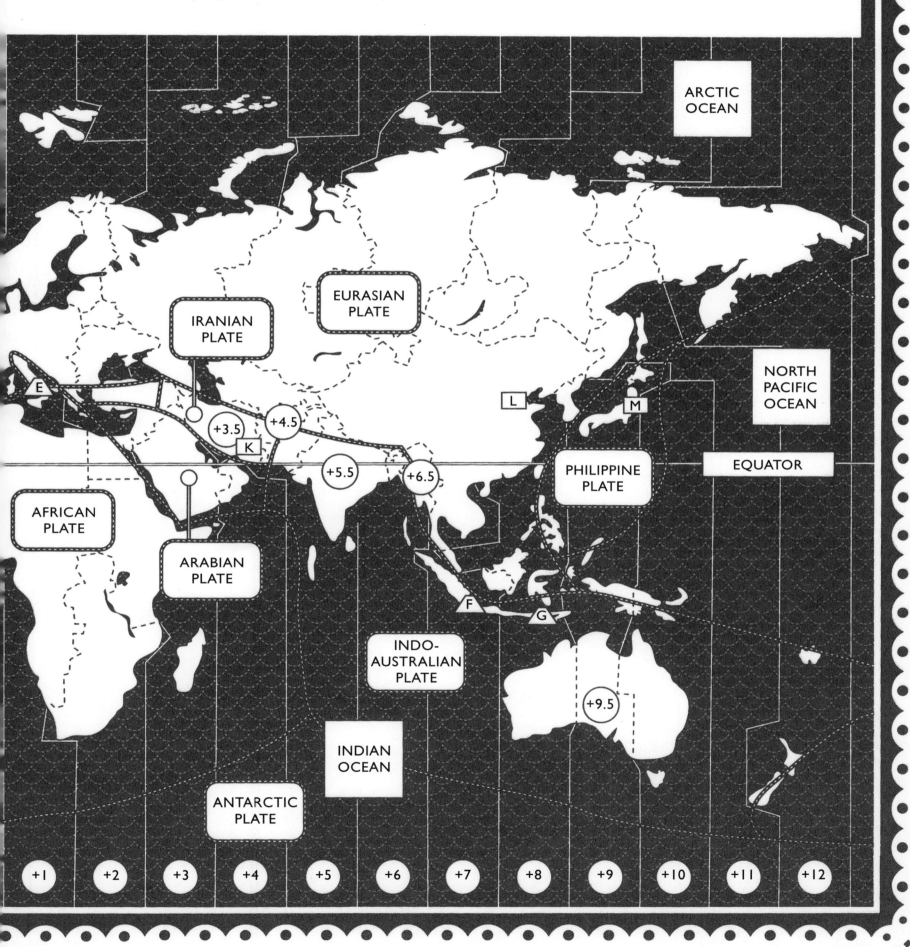

ARCTIC OCEAN

EURASIAN PLATE

IRANIAN PLATE

E

+3.5

+4.5

K

+5.5

+6.5

L

M

NORTH PACIFIC OCEAN

EQUATOR

PHILIPPINE PLATE

AFRICAN PLATE

ARABIAN PLATE

F

G

INDO-AUSTRALIAN PLATE

+9.5

INDIAN OCEAN

ANTARCTIC PLATE

+1 +2 +3 +4 +5 +6 +7 +8 +9 +10 +11 +12

THE HUMAN
EYE

As they flick alertly from left to right, our eyes are the main way in which we gather information and interpret the world. Yet turning light rays into eyesight demands a subtle mix of optics, nerves, and brain processing.

BLIND FOR A MOMENT

To stop you from getting giddy, your brain switches off your vision when your eyes move. Don't believe it? Look at your eyes in a mirror, and then look to the side and back. Did you see your eyes moving?

THE EYES HAVE IT

The edges of your field of vision are especially sensitive to movement. To prove it, gaze straight ahead, hold both arms out in front of you, and then move them apart until your hands disappear. Now wiggle your thumbs. You'll see the movement. We probably evolved this ability to alert us to predators creeping up behind us.

The six muscles that tilt and turn the eye react faster than any other human muscle.

Noticing that other animals' eyes seemed to glow in the dark, Ancient Greek thinkers believed that the human eye gave off visual "fire." The objects at which it gazed reflected the fire, making them visible. German scientist Johannes Kepler dismissed this idea. In 1604 he suggested that the eye contains a lens like that in a telescope, and that the lens focuses an image of the scene before us onto a light-sensitive retina at the back of the eye. This was already a radical idea for the time, but Kepler made another, still more amazing claim: that the image was upside-down.

To test this theory, his skeptical followers paid a visit to the butcher. Returning with bulls' eyes, they carefully peeled off the fleshy layers at the back and replaced them with eggshells. Setting the eyes in a window so that light shone through them, they saw the world outside projected on the almost-clear screen formed by the shell. And it was, indeed, upside-down.

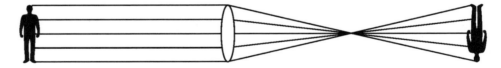

THE MIND'S EYE

How can that be, when we appear to see the world the right way up? The answer is in our brain. Our eyes are just the first stage of a very clever and complex system. The image on the retina sends electrical signals along the optic nerve to a specialized part of the brain that deals with vision. From there, nerve signals travel out to many other regions of the brain, which in turn give us the sensation of seeing the right way up.

CORRECTING OUR SIGHT

Our brains don't just flip the images from our eyes: they do much, much more. They process a torrent of imperfect information, hiding the faults and ensuring that we see (or notice) only that which is most useful. For example, there is a hole in your retina where the optic nerve connects. Your brain cleverly conceals this "blind spot," but a simple test (see below) makes it obvious.

MIND THE GAP

To find your blind spot, hold the book at arm's length and cover one eye. Gaze at the cross on the left and bring the book slowly closer. The square on the right will disappear when it falls on the blind spot.

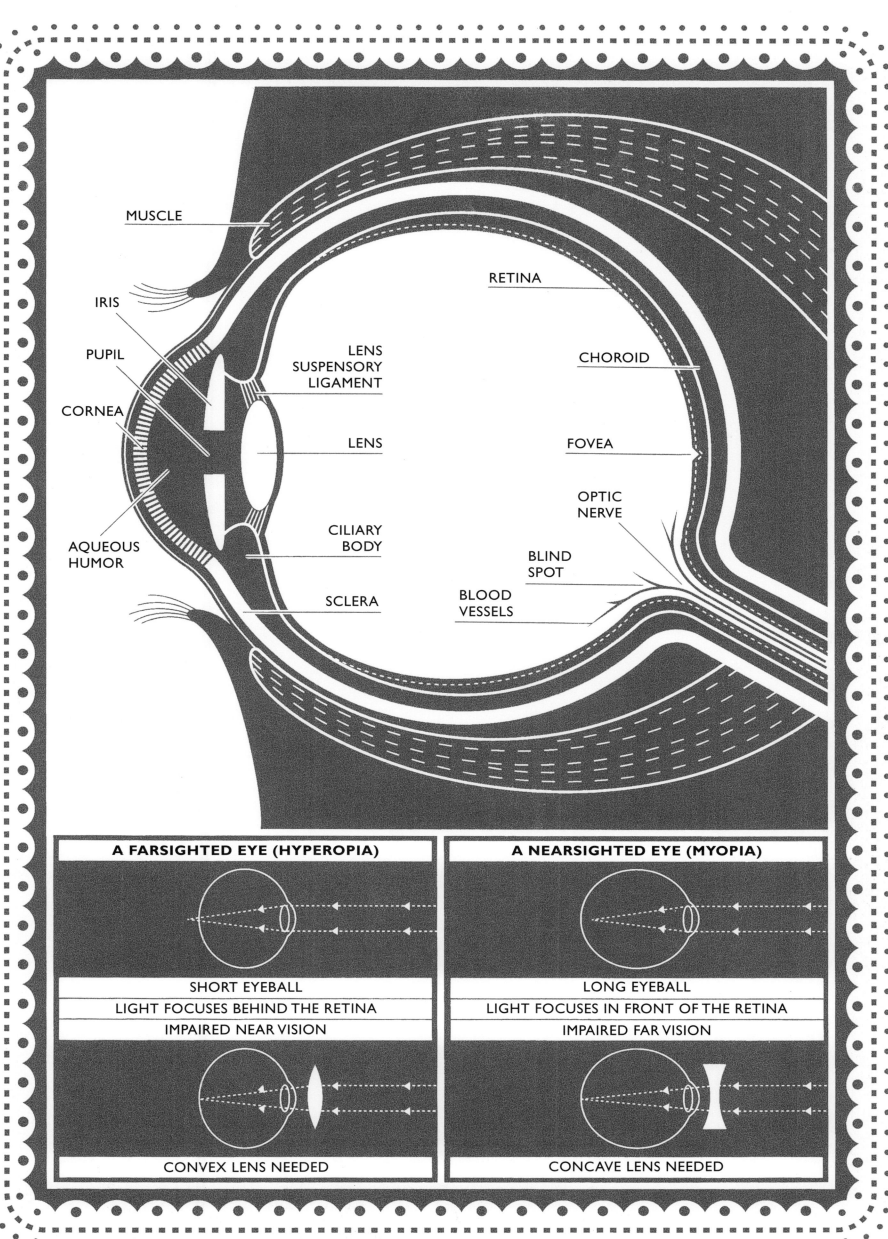

MUSCLE

IRIS

PUPIL

CORNEA

AQUEOUS
HUMOR

LENS
SUSPENSORY
LIGAMENT

LENS

CILIARY
BODY

SCLERA

RETINA

CHOROID

FOVEA

OPTIC
NERVE

BLIND
SPOT

BLOOD
VESSELS

A FARSIGHTED EYE (HYPEROPIA)

SHORT EYEBALL

LIGHT FOCUSES BEHIND THE RETINA

IMPAIRED NEAR VISION

CONVEX LENS NEEDED

A NEARSIGHTED EYE (MYOPIA)

LONG EYEBALL

LIGHT FOCUSES IN FRONT OF THE RETINA

IMPAIRED FAR VISION

CONCAVE LENS NEEDED

SHIP'S WATCH SCHEDULE
&
INTERNATIONAL CODE OF SIGNALS

The colorful flags and pennants tied to ships' rigging are not just for decoration. They send messages that sailors of any nation can understand, without the need for expert translation.

WATCH THE WATCH

A ship's crew is traditionally divided into two groups, or "watches," who take four-hour-long turns (also called watches) at working. To ensure that crew members work alternate nights, the fifth watch is split in two, to make an odd number. Bells ring each half hour to mark time during a watch; six bells, for instance, signals that three hours have passed.

DOUBLE LETTERS

Substitute flags made double letters possible without multiple sets of A–Z flags. When flown in a hoist, they signaled a repeat of the first, second, or third flag.

Sailors have always flown flags from the topmast to communicate with other vessels, but their messages used to be limited to a handful of pre-arranged signals. The British navy, for centuries the unchallenged master of the seas, tried to introduce a more versatile code in the seventeenth century. Their Fighting Instructions described a series of signals, such as this sign to attack: "As soon as they shall see the general . . . putting a red flag over the fore topmast-head . . . each squadron shall . . . engage with the enemy."

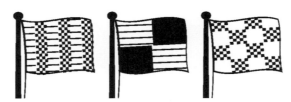

The three flags GLN signaled "I want biscuits."

TALKING CODE

More elaborate systems followed, and in 1857 the British government introduced a new International Code of Signals that greatly expanded the range of messages.

A ship carried one flag for each letter of the alphabet. The flags were rarely used to spell words. Instead, they formed a concise code that shortened long messages to "hoists" of two, three, or four flags. To send a signal, a flag officer, who was responsible for sending and interpreting signals, consulted his codebook. Arranged like a dictionary, it listed words and phrases along with the flags to signal them. For example, to ask a neighboring ship "Are there any men-of-war about?" the flag officer hauled up *C, B,* and *T* flags. *LPC* meant "What sort of bottom have you?" and *CNBT* warned of cannibalism. Place names required four flags: the Sea of Japan became *BLTS*. In all, there were 78,000 possible combinations.

BABEL FLAGS

This clever system was multilingual. (The flag officers' codebook on any given ship might be in a different language from the book used by the composers of the message.)

A version of this code is still in use, though the more colorful abbreviations are gone. When flown individually, the letter flags signal the most urgent messages. Many longer codes deal with navigation (*RJI* means "Get your engines ready as soon as possible"), while others are medical: *MSD* means "Apply cotton wool to armpit and bandage arm to side," and *MJF,* "Patient is breaking wind."

AVOIDING RUDE WORDS

The 1857 flag signals included only consonants. The British committee that compiled the code wisely decided to leave out vowels because by introducing them, "every objectionable word composed of four letters or less, not only in our own but in foreign languages, would appear in the code."

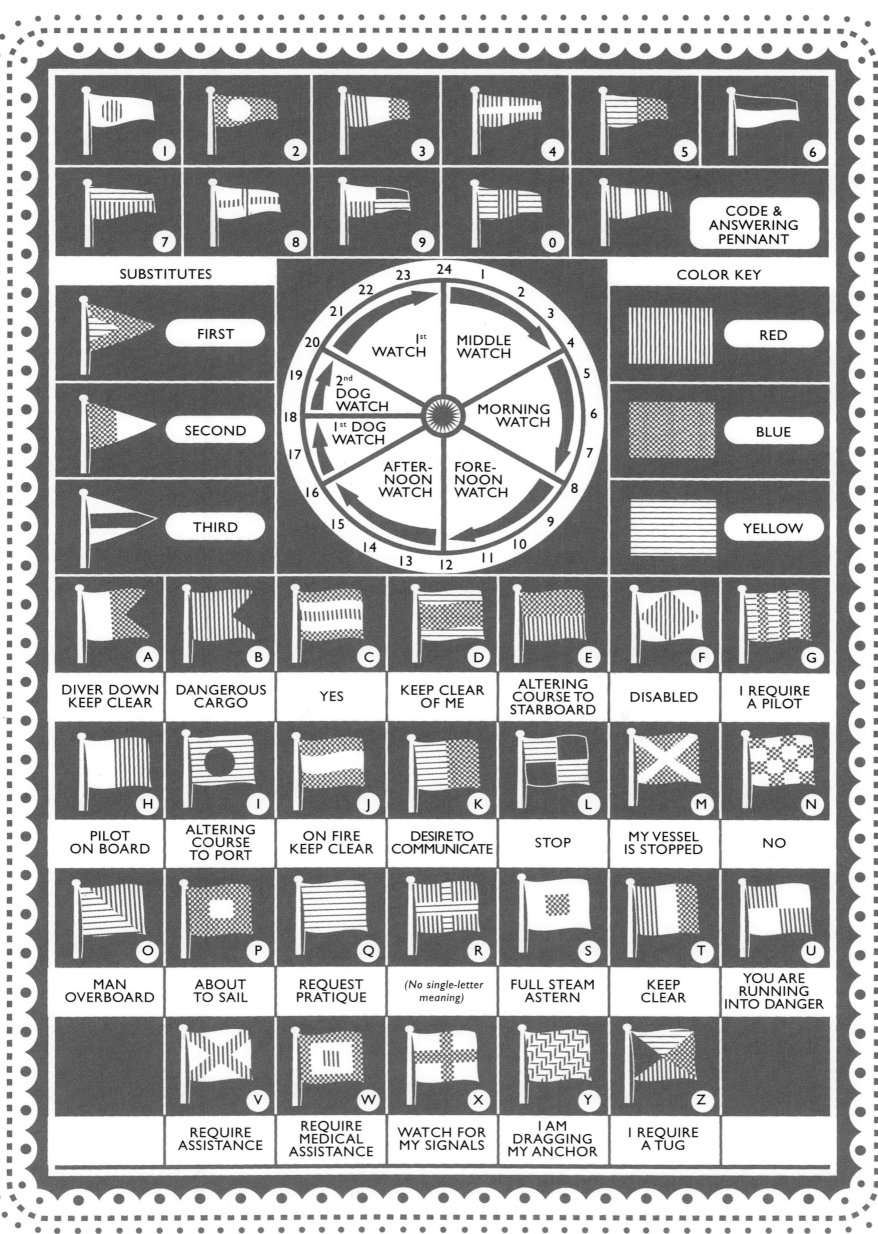

FLIGHT

Soaring with the birds was an ancient dream, but gravity rooted humans firmly to the ground until just a century ago. It was then that a pair of talented amateurs beat the experts into the air.

The ancient Greek legend that has always inspired would-be aviators is one of failure: Icarus crashed to the ground when the sun's heat melted the wax holding feathers to his makeshift wings.

This setback didn't deter the hundreds who followed him. Nicknamed "tower jumpers," their panic-stricken flapping never spared them Icarus's fate. German engineer Otto Lilienthal was among the first to make real progress. He soared on crude hang gliders . . . before he died, too, in a fatal crash in 1896.

HEAVIER THAN AIR

The Wright brothers were the first to make a heavier-than-air flying machine, but they weren't the first to fly. In 1783 French brothers Joseph-Michel and Jacques-Étienne Montgolfier launched a chicken, a duck, and a sheep into the air in a hot-air balloon. A human-crewed flight followed soon after.

The Wright brothers patented not flight itself but a method of controlling an aircraft.

WHEELS TO WINGS

Lilienthal's feats attracted the attention of a pair of brothers from Ohio. Orville and Wilbur Wright ran a bike shop but dreamed of bigger, better things. Watching buzzards riding the wind confirmed what they already suspected — that flapping wasn't the answer. So in 1900, the Wrights built a huge 16-foot-wide kite. They tested it while on vacation in North Carolina's Outer Banks, where the winds were strong and steady.

Their ingenuity was boundless. Before they built a wind tunnel (the world's first), they studied the lifting power of different wing shapes by strapping them to bicycle handlebars and pedaling full tilt down the street. Over their next few holidays, they cracked the three problems of heavier-than-air flight: lift, control, and power. Success came just before Christmas 1903.

WINNING OUTSIDERS

The Wrights beat some formidable competitors. They included British-American machine-gun tycoon Sir Hiram Maxim, and Samuel Langley, famous American scientist and director of the Smithsonian Institution. Both built planes that flopped.

WING CONTROL

Wilbur Wright figured out how to control flight while selling a customer a bicycle inner tube. Fiddling with the box, he noticed that twisting the ends changed the normally flat sides into gentle curves. Wilbur realized that if the box was the wing of a glider, air flowing over the curved surface would make it turn. Today, control surfaces such as ailerons do the same job.

RIDING ON KITES

Made of sticks, canvas, and wire, the Wrights' first "Flyer" was a fragile thing that appears to share little with the vast aircraft of today. Yet the basic principle of powered flight remains unchanged: the tear-drop curve of a wing forces air moving over it to travel faster than air flowing beneath. This creates a partial vacuum that lifts the wing and, with it, the aircraft bolted to it and the passengers inside. Familiarity has made this gravity-defying miracle commonplace — most tourists barely give it a thought when flying off to a distant beach for a couple of weeks.

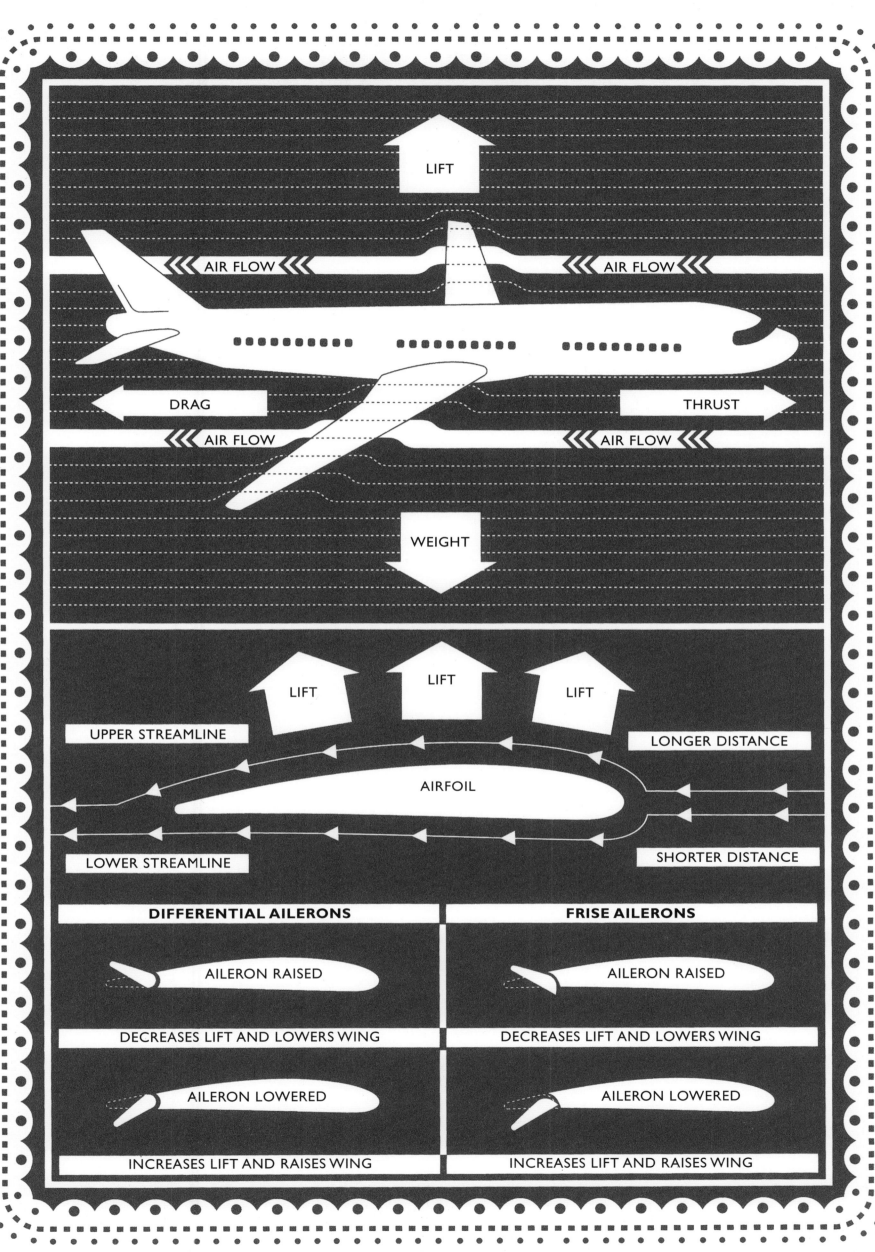

SOLSTICES and EQUINOXES

We lead such busy lives that we rarely notice daily changes in the position of sunrise and sunset. But for our ancestors, the sun's seasonal progress was a clock, a calendar, an almanac, and a prayer book.

Tilted at an angle and spinning on its axis, the earth completes an orbit of the sun every year. When our part of the earth is tilted toward the sun, we bask in long summer days; tilted away, long winter nights chill us to the bone. Exactly in between, day and night are equal. The tropics of Cancer and Capricorn are two imaginary bands encircling the earth, marking the points in the Northern and Southern hemispheres where the sun is directly overhead at midsummer noon.

TRACKING SUNRISE

Our ancient ancestors knew nothing about the earth's slow path around the sun. Instead they marked the seasons by where on the horizon the sun rose. After the shortest day of winter in the Northern Hemisphere, sunrise creeps gradually north. On the summer solstice, its progress is halted. Then the position of sunrise moves south again. Days shorten until midwinter and the beginning of a new year.

Since their crops and lives depended on it, early settlers watched this annual cycle with superstition and anxiety. The count of days from one summer or winter solstice to the next became their first calendar.

Throughout the world, monuments, temples, and observatories were built to monitor the sun's movements and time them with precision. At one of the best-known sites, England's Stonehenge, major stones and earth banks line up with sunrise at the summer solstice and with sunset at the winter solstice.

GOOD GUESS
Ancient people measured the year's length with extraordinary accuracy. A Greek astronomer named Hipparchus came up with the figure 365.24666 two thousand years ago — close enough to make a calendar that would drift by just one day every three centuries.

HIGH NOON
Between the tropics, the sun is directly overhead at noon on two days of the year, and shadows vanish beneath the objects casting them. Calendar makers used this to measure the passing years.

SUN GODS

The sun's progress has always been a holy ritual. The Aztecs thought the sun's annual cycle depended on feeding the gods with blood. To keep the sun rising each day, priests cut themselves and used stone knives to carve the beating hearts from prisoners of war. Modern festivals aren't so bloody, but we still religiously celebrate the changing seasons. Christmas falls at a time when we rejoice in the sun's midwinter return. At Easter, pagan symbols such as eggs and bunnies are a reminder of the spring rituals that preceded the Christian festival.

THE SUN

SOLSTICE (June)

EQUINOX (March)

EQUINOX (September)

SOLSTICE (December)

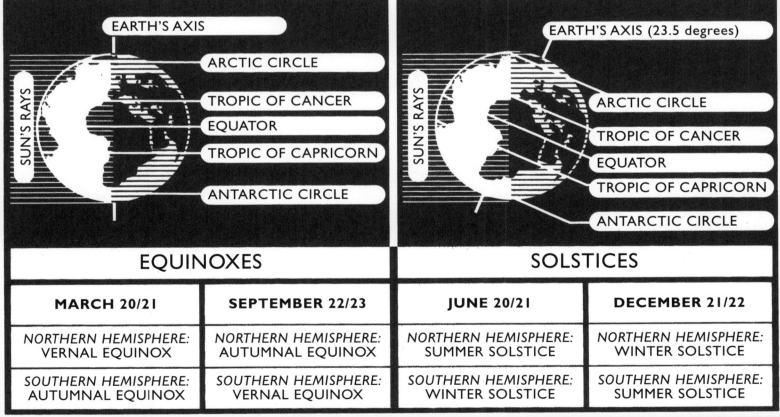

EARTH'S AXIS

ARCTIC CIRCLE

TROPIC OF CANCER

EQUATOR

TROPIC OF CAPRICORN

ANTARCTIC CIRCLE

SUN'S RAYS

EARTH'S AXIS (23.5 degrees)

ARCTIC CIRCLE

TROPIC OF CANCER

EQUATOR

TROPIC OF CAPRICORN

ANTARCTIC CIRCLE

SUN'S RAYS

EQUINOXES		SOLSTICES	
MARCH 20/21	**SEPTEMBER 22/23**	**JUNE 20/21**	**DECEMBER 21/22**
NORTHERN HEMISPHERE: VERNAL EQUINOX	*NORTHERN HEMISPHERE:* AUTUMNAL EQUINOX	*NORTHERN HEMISPHERE:* SUMMER SOLSTICE	*NORTHERN HEMISPHERE:* WINTER SOLSTICE
SOUTHERN HEMISPHERE: AUTUMNAL EQUINOX	*SOUTHERN HEMISPHERE:* VERNAL EQUINOX	*SOUTHERN HEMISPHERE:* WINTER SOLSTICE	*SOUTHERN HEMISPHERE:* SUMMER SOLSTICE

RIVERS

The world's great cities were all built beside rivers. River water quenches our thirst, irrigates our crops, provides us with power and transportation, and removes our waste.

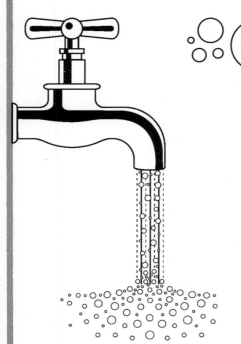

Cascading down from a mountain source or meandering to the sea, rivers are inspiring—and vital. Powerful cities have grown up on their banks: not only were they a source of drinking water for the first settlers, rivers could be both transportation arteries for citizens and formidable barriers for travelers. Either way, they were worth protecting. Pittsburgh, for instance, commands the confluence of the Allegheny and Monongahela Rivers, which forms the Ohio River; the city of Bordeaux in France guards the lowest point where the Garonne River was narrow enough to bridge.

EROSION AND DEPOSITION

As a river carves up the landscape, it creates imposing natural fortresses, as in Quebec, where the Saint Lawrence River curves around a high bluff. And as a river slows and winds, its silt makes plains and deltas, where crops thrive. Famously, the ancient Egyptians grew food on the banks of the Nile and drank its water. The Nile still reaches the sea, but not all rivers do the same: we use so much water that many of the world's rivers regularly run dry. Bitter conflict threatens as nations squabble for the biggest share of water that flows across borders.

WORKING WITH WATER

We need to make better use of rivers, but doing more requires tough or distasteful decisions. Already, treatment plants turn upstream sewage into downstream drinking water. In a dozen cities worldwide, more than half of each glass is recycled effluent. "Replumbing" rivers to direct their flow where it's needed is a popular solution with politicians: China's "South-to-North" plan will send the waters of the Yangtze to fill the Yellow River. However, schemes like this threaten dire environmental consequences. Grassroots campaigners instead favor low-tech water management, such as the neglected gabarbands (low-walled community dams) of Balochistan, in Pakistan. Rejuvenated there and copied elsewhere, they could help quench our thirst without harming wildlife.

FIRST RIVER CITIES
Civilization began on a riverbank: the world's first cities grew up along the Indus River, in what is now Pakistan, 5,300 years ago.

ANYONE FOR A BATH?
The ancient Romans were experts at managing rivers. Eleven aqueducts fed the city of Rome: the Anio Novus channeled water there from the Aniene River 22 miles away. In the streets, there was running water from free public taps, and in CE 100, everyone in Rome had as much water as each person in New York had in 1900.

By 2025, a third of the world's population may face water shortages.

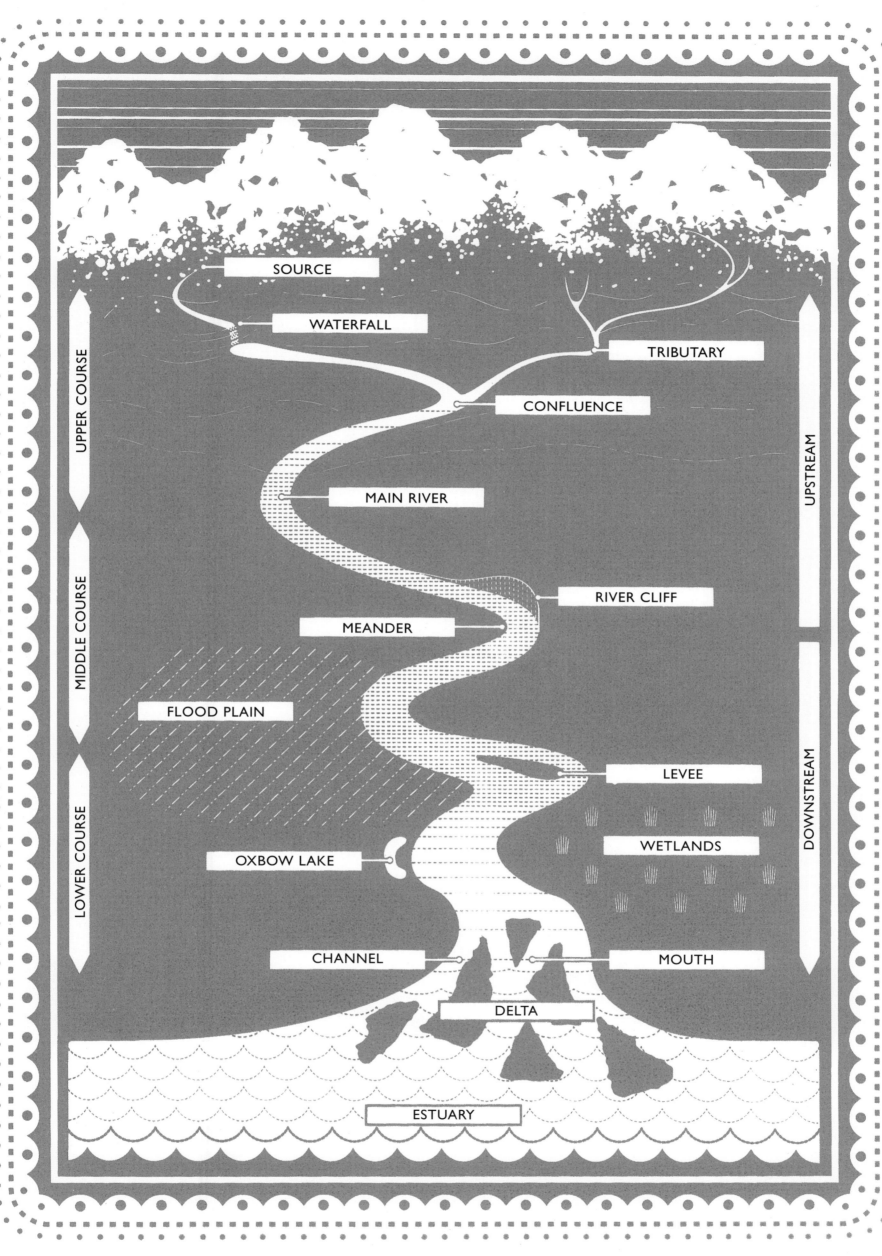

SOURCE

WATERFALL

TRIBUTARY

CONFLUENCE

UPPER COURSE

UPSTREAM

MAIN RIVER

MIDDLE COURSE

RIVER CLIFF

MEANDER

FLOOD PLAIN

DOWNSTREAM

LEVEE

LOWER COURSE

WETLANDS

OXBOW LAKE

CHANNEL

MOUTH

DELTA

ESTUARY

PERIODIC TABLE
of the
ELEMENTS

In ancient times, there were four "elements": earth, air, fire, and water. Now we know that life isn't so simple. There are nearly one hundred different pure chemicals, which combine to make every natural thing. The periodic table arranges them by their properties.

33 As

the centuries passed, the number of known elements increased: by 1500, the list was thirteen. Over the next 350 years, another forty-five were discovered. Many had shared properties, and chemists started listing similar elements, arranging them in neat horizontal lines called periods. In the nineteenth century, efforts were made to group the elements by property so that they could be better understood. Chemists listed elements by the weight of a single atom of that element. When organized by atomic weight, several similar elements would line up neatly, so they knew they were on the right track.

Then Russian chemistry professor Dmitry Mendeleyev looked at the problem while writing a university textbook. On a frosty day in February 1869 he began to plan chapters of the book by grouping elements together. By the end of three days, he had arranged the elements in orderly rows and columns, but still had no complete solution.

76 Os

Osmium (76) is the smelly element: it gets its name from the Greek word osmē, meaning "smell," because it gives off an unpleasant odor when heated.

He worked on through the next day, canceling an appointment to speak at a cheese makers convention. That afternoon, he slumped exhausted on his desk and fell into a deep sleep. He awoke astonished: "I saw in a dream a table where all the elements fell into place as required." He groggily rushed to draw it.

Mendeleyev again listed the elements in rows by weight. This time, though, he shifted the rows, so that elements with similar properties lined up in columns. But to get the arrangement to fit, he had to cheat. He left gaps, predicting new elements with properties halfway between those on either side. He also swapped elements to make them work in his scheme.

The periodic table is still growing: elements 113, 115, 117, and 118 were added at the end of 2015.

TRIUMPH!

Scientists scoffed when Mendeleyev announced his discovery the following month, but six years later, a French chemist discovered gallium (31), filling the gap between aluminum (13) and uranium (92). Its properties and weight were exactly as Mendeleyev had predicted!

Mendeleyev's other spark of brilliance was his tinkering with the order. We now know that each element owes its properties to its atomic number — the count of protons whizzing around its nucleus (see pages 16–17). Sorting by atomic number instead of weight produces a slightly different order.

NOW YOU SEE IT

Only ninety-eight known elements occur in nature. Scientists isolate new ones by speeding up the atoms of one element in a particle accelerator (a huge circle of magnets), which slams them into a target made of another element. To make meitnerium (109), German scientists fired iron (26) atoms at bismuth (83) for a week. They made just one atom of the new element — but it decayed in 0.005 seconds.

27 Co

FAIRY ELEMENT

Cobalt (27) is named from the German word for goblin (Kobold). Sixteenth-century silver miners heated cobalt ore, expecting it to turn to silver (47). When it instead gave off deadly arsenic (33) vapor, they decided it had been cursed by goblins.

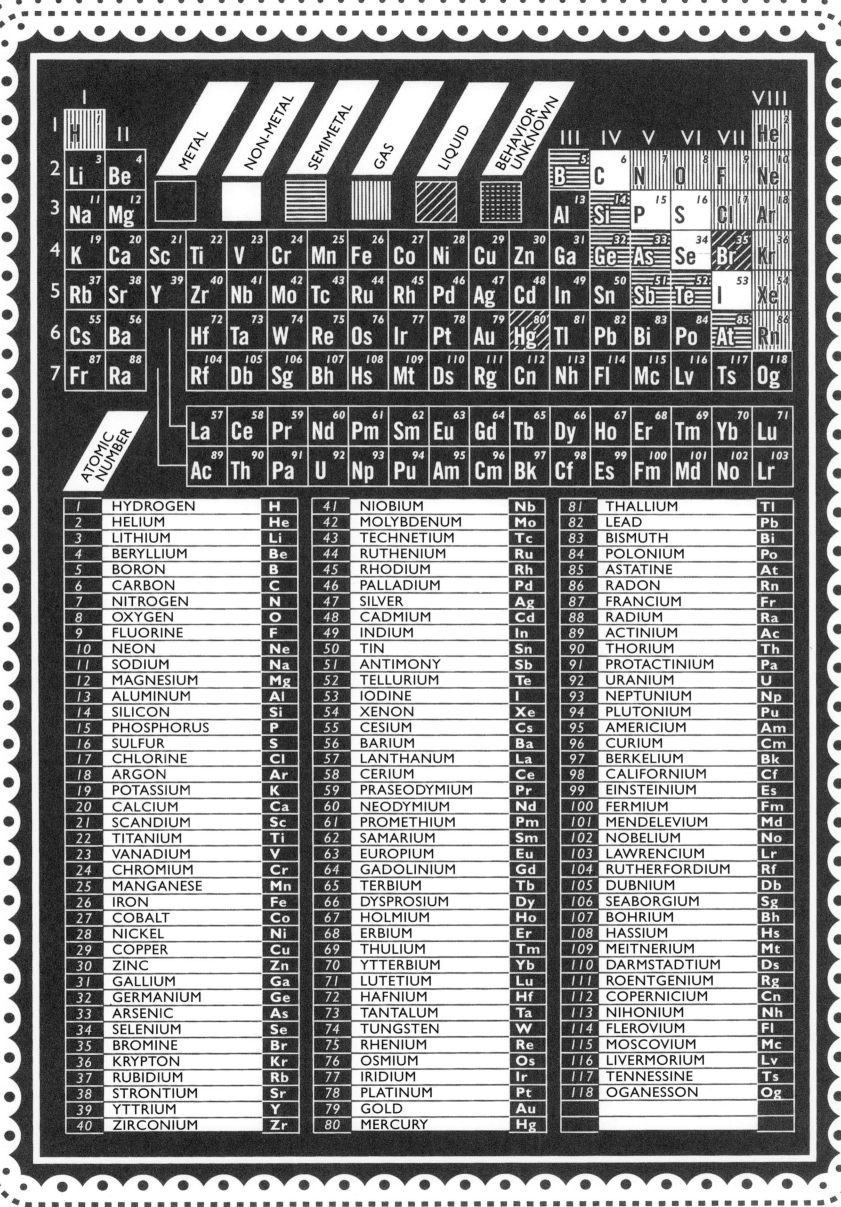

#	Element	Symbol	#	Element	Symbol	#	Element	Symbol
1	HYDROGEN	H	41	NIOBIUM	Nb	81	THALLIUM	Tl
2	HELIUM	He	42	MOLYBDENUM	Mo	82	LEAD	Pb
3	LITHIUM	Li	43	TECHNETIUM	Tc	83	BISMUTH	Bi
4	BERYLLIUM	Be	44	RUTHENIUM	Ru	84	POLONIUM	Po
5	BORON	B	45	RHODIUM	Rh	85	ASTATINE	At
6	CARBON	C	46	PALLADIUM	Pd	86	RADON	Rn
7	NITROGEN	N	47	SILVER	Ag	87	FRANCIUM	Fr
8	OXYGEN	O	48	CADMIUM	Cd	88	RADIUM	Ra
9	FLUORINE	F	49	INDIUM	In	89	ACTINIUM	Ac
10	NEON	Ne	50	TIN	Sn	90	THORIUM	Th
11	SODIUM	Na	51	ANTIMONY	Sb	91	PROTACTINIUM	Pa
12	MAGNESIUM	Mg	52	TELLURIUM	Te	92	URANIUM	U
13	ALUMINUM	Al	53	IODINE	I	93	NEPTUNIUM	Np
14	SILICON	Si	54	XENON	Xe	94	PLUTONIUM	Pu
15	PHOSPHORUS	P	55	CESIUM	Cs	95	AMERICIUM	Am
16	SULFUR	S	56	BARIUM	Ba	96	CURIUM	Cm
17	CHLORINE	Cl	57	LANTHANUM	La	97	BERKELIUM	Bk
18	ARGON	Ar	58	CERIUM	Ce	98	CALIFORNIUM	Cf
19	POTASSIUM	K	59	PRASEODYMIUM	Pr	99	EINSTEINIUM	Es
20	CALCIUM	Ca	60	NEODYMIUM	Nd	100	FERMIUM	Fm
21	SCANDIUM	Sc	61	PROMETHIUM	Pm	101	MENDELEVIUM	Md
22	TITANIUM	Ti	62	SAMARIUM	Sm	102	NOBELIUM	No
23	VANADIUM	V	63	EUROPIUM	Eu	103	LAWRENCIUM	Lr
24	CHROMIUM	Cr	64	GADOLINIUM	Gd	104	RUTHERFORDIUM	Rf
25	MANGANESE	Mn	65	TERBIUM	Tb	105	DUBNIUM	Db
26	IRON	Fe	66	DYSPROSIUM	Dy	106	SEABORGIUM	Sg
27	COBALT	Co	67	HOLMIUM	Ho	107	BOHRIUM	Bh
28	NICKEL	Ni	68	ERBIUM	Er	108	HASSIUM	Hs
29	COPPER	Cu	69	THULIUM	Tm	109	MEITNERIUM	Mt
30	ZINC	Zn	70	YTTERBIUM	Yb	110	DARMSTADTIUM	Ds
31	GALLIUM	Ga	71	LUTETIUM	Lu	111	ROENTGENIUM	Rg
32	GERMANIUM	Ge	72	HAFNIUM	Hf	112	COPERNICIUM	Cn
33	ARSENIC	As	73	TANTALUM	Ta	113	NIHONIUM	Nh
34	SELENIUM	Se	74	TUNGSTEN	W	114	FLEROVIUM	Fl
35	BROMINE	Br	75	RHENIUM	Re	115	MOSCOVIUM	Mc
36	KRYPTON	Kr	76	OSMIUM	Os	116	LIVERMORIUM	Lv
37	RUBIDIUM	Rb	77	IRIDIUM	Ir	117	TENNESSINE	Ts
38	STRONTIUM	Sr	78	PLATINUM	Pt	118	OGANESSON	Og
39	YTTRIUM	Y	79	GOLD	Au			
40	ZIRCONIUM	Zr	80	MERCURY	Hg			

PENCILS & BRUSHES
FOR THE ARTIST AND DESIGNER

The most ancient of artists' tools, brushes were first used to paint cave walls nearly 40,000 years ago. Upstart pencils had to wait for the discovery of graphite in the early sixteenth century.

Home decoration began with finger painting, but when cave artists needed a finer line than a fingerprint could provide, they separated the fibers of twigs to turn them into brushes. Later they painted with hair, or the fur of horse, goat, deer, fox, and even wolf.

Even though we call them "sable," the softest brushes are no longer made from the fur of this rare Russian animal; Siberian weasels supply the bristles instead. Until the nineteenth century, these bristles were held inside the hollow shaft of a bird's feather, which limited brush shapes. But fastening them to wooden handles with a band (or "ferrule") of tin or silver allowed nineteenth-century brush makers to create new brush shapes like the fan, as the band could be bent into different designs.

Legend has it that a schoolgirl from Massachusetts made the first American pencil before 1800 by mixing crushed graphite and glue in an alder-twig holder.

Before the discovery of graphite, thin strips of lead were used to draw faint gray lines. The middle of a pencil is still called a lead, even though there's no real lead in it.

DYING FOR PENCILS
Pencils became scarce after Britain's generals discovered that newly cast cannonballs were easier to remove from their molds if they were painted with graphite. Smuggling graphite was a felony, punishable by hanging.

NAMING BRUSHES
Some brushes are named after objects they resemble or for the job they do. The "filbert" brush looks like a hazelnut, which was called "Saint Philbert's nut" in Old French. In marine paintings, the long-haired "rigger" brush was used to add the fine detail of ships' rigging.

GRAPHITE TO PENCIL
The pencil was named after a narrow brush, and early examples were called "dry pencils" to distinguish them from the wet, furry version. Pencils seem such an obvious idea that we hardly think of them as an invention. Yet when graphite was first discovered at Borrowdale in England in the early sixteenth century, nobody appreciated its value—except local shepherds, who used it to mark their flocks. By 1565, artists and carpenters were buying graphite sawed into sticks and wrapped in string.

WHO WAS FIRST?
Nobody knows for sure who first thought of fixing strips of graphite inside little wooden sticks to make them easy to sharpen and hold in the hand. There's an English tradition that a carpenter living near Borrowdale was the first, but there are German competitors. The Nuremberg carpenters' guild had the exclusive rights to pencil making, and in 1662 Friedrich Staedtler started a pencil factory in the same city.

It was the French who turned graphite into the modern pencil. In 1794, balloonist and army officer Nicolas-Jacques Conté mixed graphite and clay to make pencil "leads" that wrote smoothly. Better yet, he made them in grades of hardness and blackness. Pencils have hardly changed to this day.

MM CM 1 2 3 4 5 6 7 8 9 10 11 12 13 14 15
INCH 1 2 3 4 5 6

RIGGER

BRIGHT

FILBERT

ANGLE

ROUND

FLAT

FAN

MOP

HARDER

SOFTER

9H 8H 7H 6H 5H

5B 6B 7B 8B 9B

4H

3H

2H

4B

3B

#4

#3

#2½

#2

#1

2B

H

F

HB

B

PRIMARY RED

TERTIARY RED-ORANGE

TERTIARY VIOLET-RED

SECONDARY ORANGE

SECONDARY VIOLET

TERTIARY ORANGE-YELLOW

TERTIARY BLUE-VIOLET

SECONDARY ORANGE

SECONDARY VIOLET

PRIMARY RED

PRIMARY YELLOW

PRIMARY BLUE

PRIMARY YELLOW

PRIMARY BLUE

TERTIARY YELLOW-GREEN

SECONDARY GREEN

SECONDARY GREEN

TERTIARY GREEN-BLUE

TECHNICAL DRAWING

GENERAL LAYOUT

FREEHAND DRAWING

47

THE PHASES OF
THE MOON

Over the course of its monthly circuit around the earth, the moon seems to swell from a thin sliver to a brilliant ball before shrinking away to nothing. These nightly changing phases have inspired awe, science, and superstition.

The moon's phases are nothing more than a trick of the light. Earth's companion satellite doesn't really change its size and shape. It's the changing position of the moon relative to the earth and the sun that affect how much illuminated moon we see.

The moon's circling path around the earth causes the lunar phases, which repeat every 29.5 days. The regular, and therefore predictable, return of the full moon gave rise to some of the earliest calendars some 10,000 years ago. It also accounts for our twelve-month year (though dividing 365 by 29.5 required a bit of cheating by the calendar's Roman inventors).

HARVEST MOON
Usually moonrise is fifty minutes later each day, but around the autumnal equinox (see pages 40–41), an almost full moon rises soon after sunset several nights in a row. This "harvest moon" lights the fields for those gathering crops. A full moon rising soon after sunset makes it possible to continue outdoor work into the evening.

Before electric power, the full moon's light was essential to guide night travelers.

LUNAR LEGENDS

There is a wealth of folklore based on the moon's phases. As recently as the 1920s, Austrian philosopher Rudolf Steiner proposed that planting seeds at particular phases of the moon made crops grow stronger. The most persistent myth is that the full moon makes mental illness worse. In the past, people with psychiatric disorders were called "lunatics" and constrained at full moon.

The full moon doesn't affect people's brains, but belief in the mystical effects of the moon is so pervasive that people can trick themselves into thinking otherwise. Some midwives claim they deliver more babies when the moon is full, but this simply isn't the case. Equally, some police commanders put more cops on the beat because they fear a crime wave at the full moon, even though, in reality, a crime is no more likely to occur at this time of the month than at any other.

ONCE IN A BLUE MOON
Most years there are twelve cycles of moon phases. But since this takes only 354 days, there is an "extra" full moon, called a blue moon, once every two or three years. So, despite the traditional idiom, "once in a blue moon" is not really rare at all.

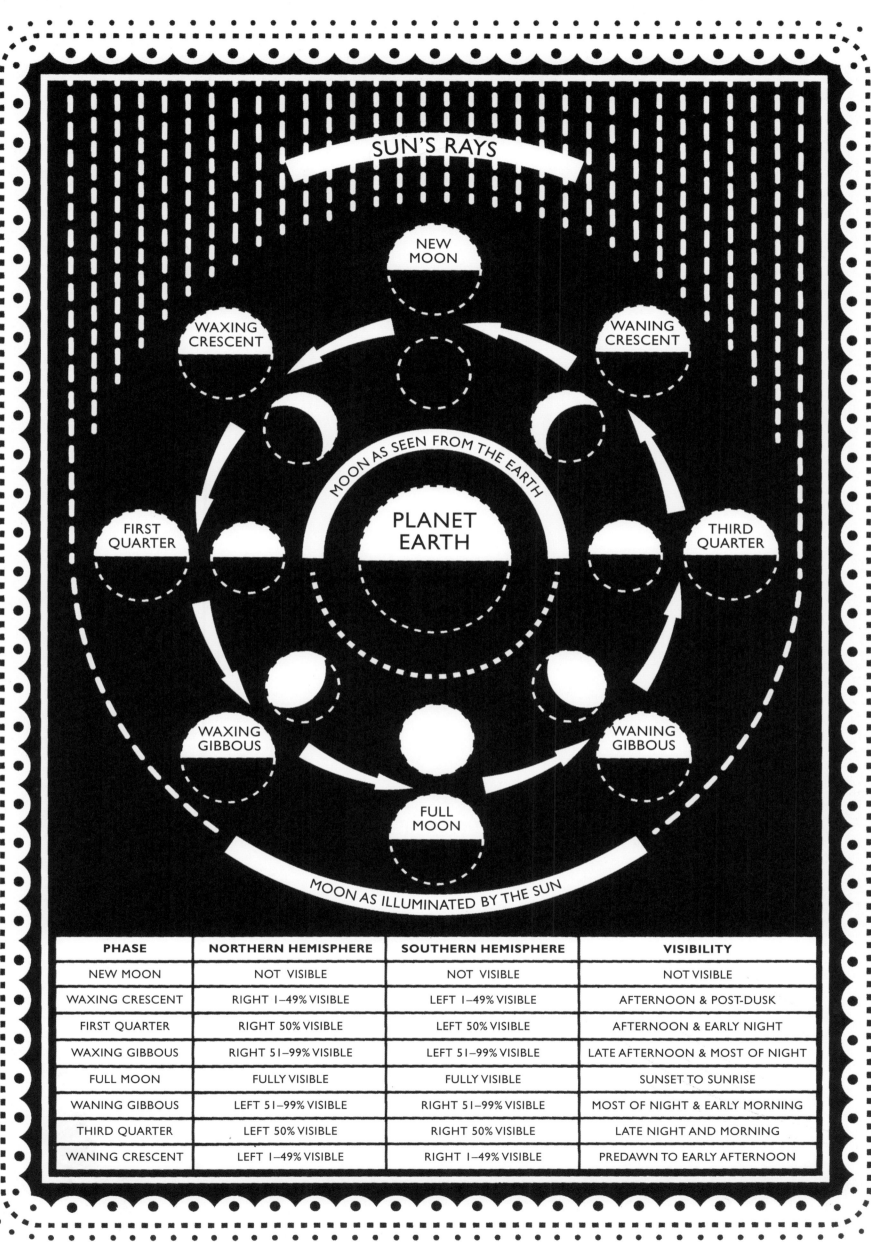

PHASE	NORTHERN HEMISPHERE	SOUTHERN HEMISPHERE	VISIBILITY
NEW MOON	NOT VISIBLE	NOT VISIBLE	NOT VISIBLE
WAXING CRESCENT	RIGHT 1–49% VISIBLE	LEFT 1–49% VISIBLE	AFTERNOON & POST-DUSK
FIRST QUARTER	RIGHT 50% VISIBLE	LEFT 50% VISIBLE	AFTERNOON & EARLY NIGHT
WAXING GIBBOUS	RIGHT 51–99% VISIBLE	LEFT 51–99% VISIBLE	LATE AFTERNOON & MOST OF NIGHT
FULL MOON	FULLY VISIBLE	FULLY VISIBLE	SUNSET TO SUNRISE
WANING GIBBOUS	LEFT 51–99% VISIBLE	RIGHT 51–99% VISIBLE	MOST OF NIGHT & EARLY MORNING
THIRD QUARTER	LEFT 50% VISIBLE	RIGHT 50% VISIBLE	LATE NIGHT AND MORNING
WANING CRESCENT	LEFT 1–49% VISIBLE	RIGHT 1–49% VISIBLE	PREDAWN TO EARLY AFTERNOON

ORGANS
OF THE
BODY

Respect for the dead kept us ignorant about our organs until around three hundred years ago. Before then, physicians learned anatomy from the bodies of animals, executed criminals, and those injured in battle.

Since warfare began some 14,000 years ago, battlefields have provided vivid, if gruesome, glimpses of the organs that keep our bodies working. The warrior's sword opened the belly in an instant and showed, for example, that the gut was a single winding tunnel with two open ends.

To learn more, first-century Indian anatomists left corpses to rot and examined them using brushes. In Greece, fourth-century-BCE physician Herophilos cut open criminals before and after execution; a few centuries later, Greek surgeon Galen studied the injuries of wounded gladiators.

BAFFLING BODIES

Their work enabled physicians to describe the organs of the body but not to understand them. For example, they noticed we experience hunger when our stomachs are empty, but they couldn't explain why.

Other organs proved equally baffling, among them the liver. It was recognized in ancient times as one of the body's three vital organs, along with the brain and heart. Galen thought its job was to make blood and to warm the stomach. He also spotted the spleen and gallbladder, and he guessed that both played a part in digestion. But he was limited by his desire to make all the organs conform to the "theory of humors." According to this popular system, good health relied on the balance of four fluids: blood, phlegm, yellow bile, and black bile.

This delusion held back the study of the body for thirteen centuries. Anatomists grew skilled at drawing and describing the organs, but their understanding scarcely improved. As late as 1500, they still believed the lungs controlled anger.

YOU MUST BE JOKING
Though William Harvey's discoveries about the heart were a breakthrough in anatomy, he still clung to ancient beliefs. He claimed the ability to laugh was a sign of a healthy spleen: according to the theory of humors, it regulated melancholia.

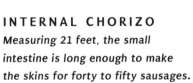

INTERNAL CHORIZO
Measuring 21 feet, the small intestine is long enough to make the skins for forty to fifty sausages.

"Ancient ideas about the heart regulating emotions have been proven false, yet we still call romances "affairs of the heart."

DAWN OF SCIENCE

This ignorance ended with the rise of modern science in the seventeenth century. In 1628, English physician William Harvey recognized the role of the heart in circulating blood. The other organs gradually revealed their secrets to inquisitive scalpels and newly invented microscopes.

The last and enduring mystery is the brain. Though its microscopic structures had been extensively studied by the end of the nineteenth century, we still cannot explain how its 100 billion nerve cells give us consciousness, personality, or happiness.

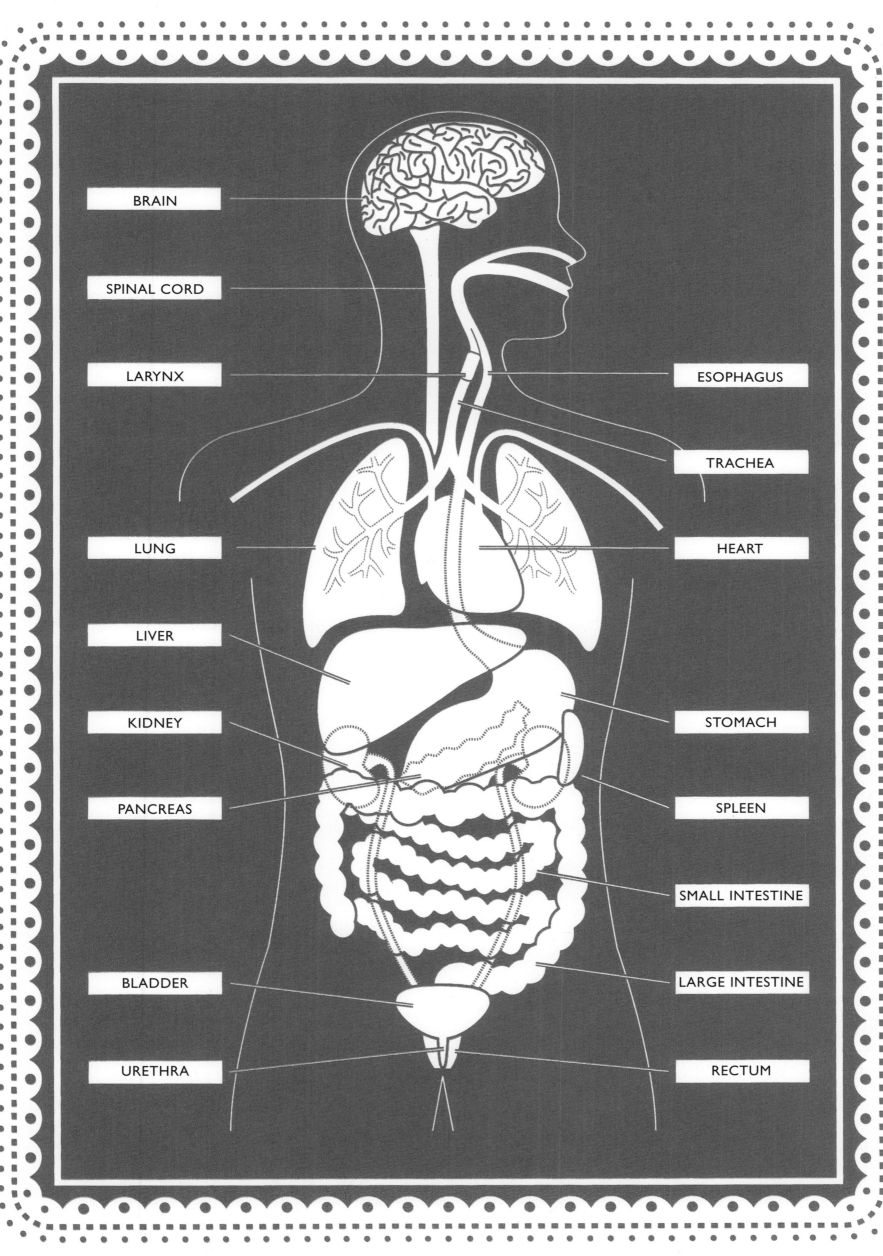

BRAIN

SPINAL CORD

LARYNX

ESOPHAGUS

TRACHEA

LUNG

HEART

LIVER

KIDNEY

STOMACH

PANCREAS

SPLEEN

SMALL INTESTINE

BLADDER

LARGE INTESTINE

URETHRA

RECTUM

REGULAR POLYGONS

We call many-sided shapes that have equal angles and identical sides "regular polygons." Those with the fewest sides widely occur in nature and have common names, but there are mathematical names for every single one.

To find the most elegant example of regular polygons in the natural world, look in a hive. Honeybees evolved to build their combs in hexagons, because these pack exactly together and use the least wax in covering the largest surface area.

The thin wax of a honeycomb is surprisingly hard to break, so we humans copy the bees, valuing hive-like hexagons for their strength and economy of materials. You'll find hexagonal structures in everything from cardboard packaging to composite aircraft wings.

Human interest in regular polygons is as old as mathematics itself: in ancient Greece, during the fourth century BCE, Plato suggested that everything in the physical universe was made up of regular polygons. Our modern names for these shapes are all in the Greek language, once you get past triangles and quadrilaterals. Every one ends in *-gon,* from the Greek word for "angle," and mathematicians string together Greek number names to count the edges.

The names rapidly turn into tongue-twisters as the number of sides increases. For instance, a forty-nine-sided regular polygon is a tetracontaenneagon. Mathematicians even have names for one- and two-sided figures — monogons and digons — though they struggle to describe them in a way that most of us can understand!

NATURAL POLYGONS

It's not just living things that create regular polygons — they are common in geology, too. Shining crystals and volcanic rocks make these pleasing regular shapes because their atoms (see pages 16–17) behave like spheres. They stack up in regular lines and rows, just as identical apples piled in a fruit stall form a neat pyramid.

The Giant's Causeway in Northern Ireland's County Antrim is entirely natural. Most of its 40,000 basalt columns are hexagonal, though there are also square and octagonal columns. Formed from lava some 60 million years ago, it's perhaps the world's most famous tiled pavement.

Ancient Greek mathematicians knew how to construct polygons with three, four, and five sides using only a compass and ruler.

108°

90°

TILING
Hexagons fit together neatly in a pattern that completely covers a flat surface — a quality we call tiling. Besides hexagons, only squares and triangles do this on their own. Regular polygons with more sides can do it, too, if you don't restrict their pattern to a single variety.

A polygon with an infinite number of sides is a circle.

ISLAMIC MOSAICS
The intricately tiled walls of Islamic architecture take this geometry to a decorative extreme. This style is called girih: the earliest known examples of this tiling appeared circa 1200.

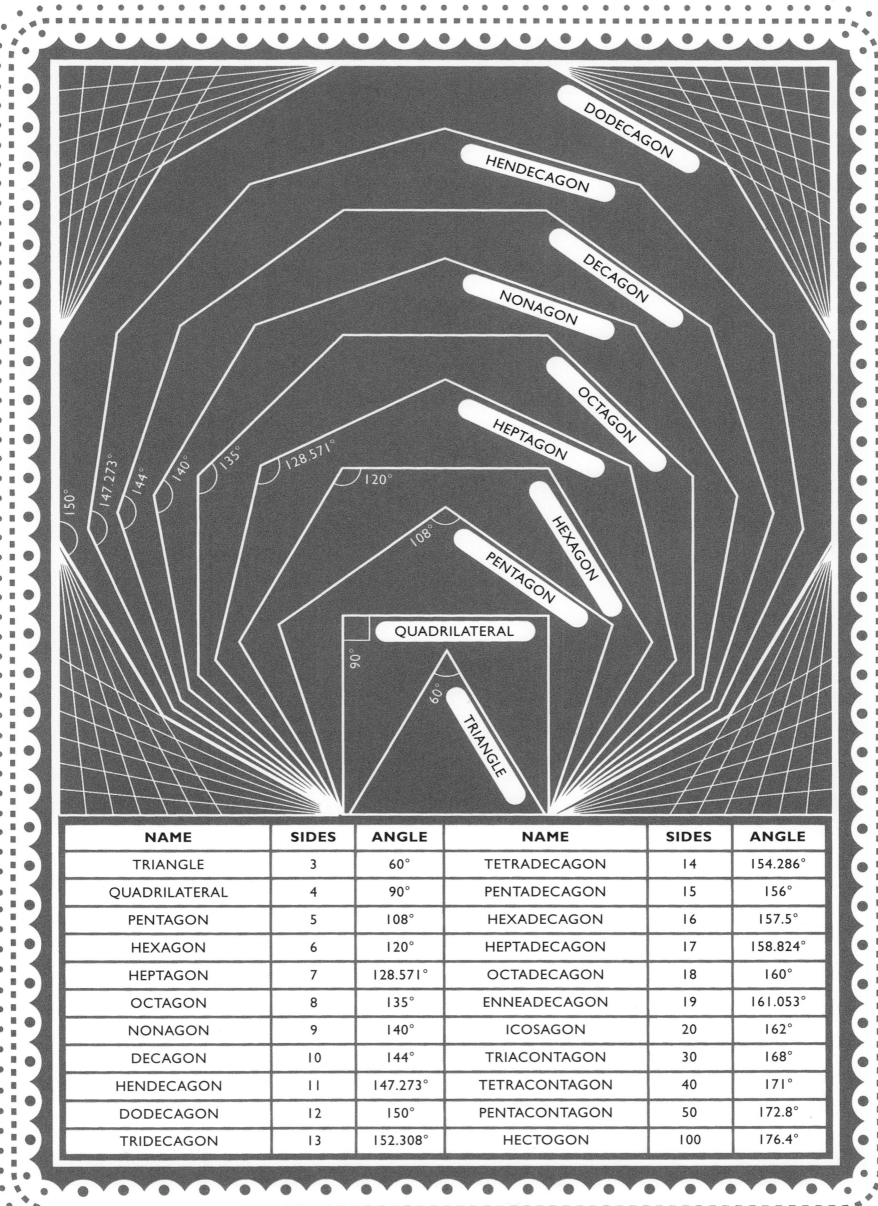

NAME	SIDES	ANGLE	NAME	SIDES	ANGLE
TRIANGLE	3	60°	TETRADECAGON	14	154.286°
QUADRILATERAL	4	90°	PENTADECAGON	15	156°
PENTAGON	5	108°	HEXADECAGON	16	157.5°
HEXAGON	6	120°	HEPTADECAGON	17	158.824°
HEPTAGON	7	128.571°	OCTADECAGON	18	160°
OCTAGON	8	135°	ENNEADECAGON	19	161.053°
NONAGON	9	140°	ICOSAGON	20	162°
DECAGON	10	144°	TRIACONTAGON	30	168°
HENDECAGON	11	147.273°	TETRACONTAGON	40	171°
DODECAGON	12	150°	PENTACONTAGON	50	172.8°
TRIDECAGON	13	152.308°	HECTOGON	100	176.4°

THE LAYOUT
of an
ORCHESTRA

The arrangement of instruments in a classical concert orchestra seems like a traditional standard, but it is far more changeable than one might imagine — and it has a remarkably short history.

Music is ancient, but orchestras are not. Until the early seventeenth century, European musicians rarely played in large groups. When they were summoned for dances and feasts, or to accompany opera and ballet, players had no fixed seats: they just fit themselves into the available space. A "standard" pattern began to emerge in eighteenth-century operas, but it was unlike today's: violinists faced one another in two rows . . . at double-sided desks!

KEEPING THE BEAT

In small groups, musicians had no problem keeping time because they could hear one another's notes. However, as numbers grew, they needed a leader they could see and follow.

In casual playing, they formed a circle around the harpsichordist or the leading violinist. But in formal performances, musicians had to face the audience, so the circle became a crescent. Starting in France, leaders abandoned their instruments, synchronizing their orchestras as "time beaters."

By the 1820s, they had taken center stage and become conductors, controlling all aspects of performances — including where musicians sat. They arranged instruments according to the demands of the music, making sure that no one group dominated the sound. That's why they put percussionists, with their loud drums and cymbals, at the back.

DANGEROUS PROFESSION

French composer Jean-Baptiste Lully was banging a large stick on the floor to beat time for an orchestra in 1687 when he accidentally struck and injured his foot. He died of the wound three months later.

BOOM, BOOM!

There was no place for double basses in the orchestra until the early eighteenth century; when they were first introduced, composers used them only for special effects such as thunder and earthquakes.

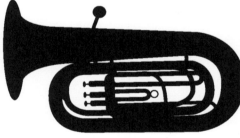

French composer Hector Berlioz wrote that members of an orchestra are intelligent machines that the conductor plays like an immense piano.

THERE IS NO STANDARD

Today the "standard" plan shown opposite is flexible, and conductors adapt it for different-shaped stages, or to fit in extra instruments as the score requires. The piano is the most obvious example: it's often at the front of the stage, with the strings shuffling sideways to make room.

Modern music sometimes employs instruments that Bach and Beethoven never dreamed of, and these require novel arrangements of the stage. For example, Malcolm Arnold's 1956 *A Grand, Grand Overture* needs three vacuum cleaners and a floor polisher. When it was performed at London's Royal Albert Hall in 2008, the instruments were slotted in at the front of the stage next to the violins.

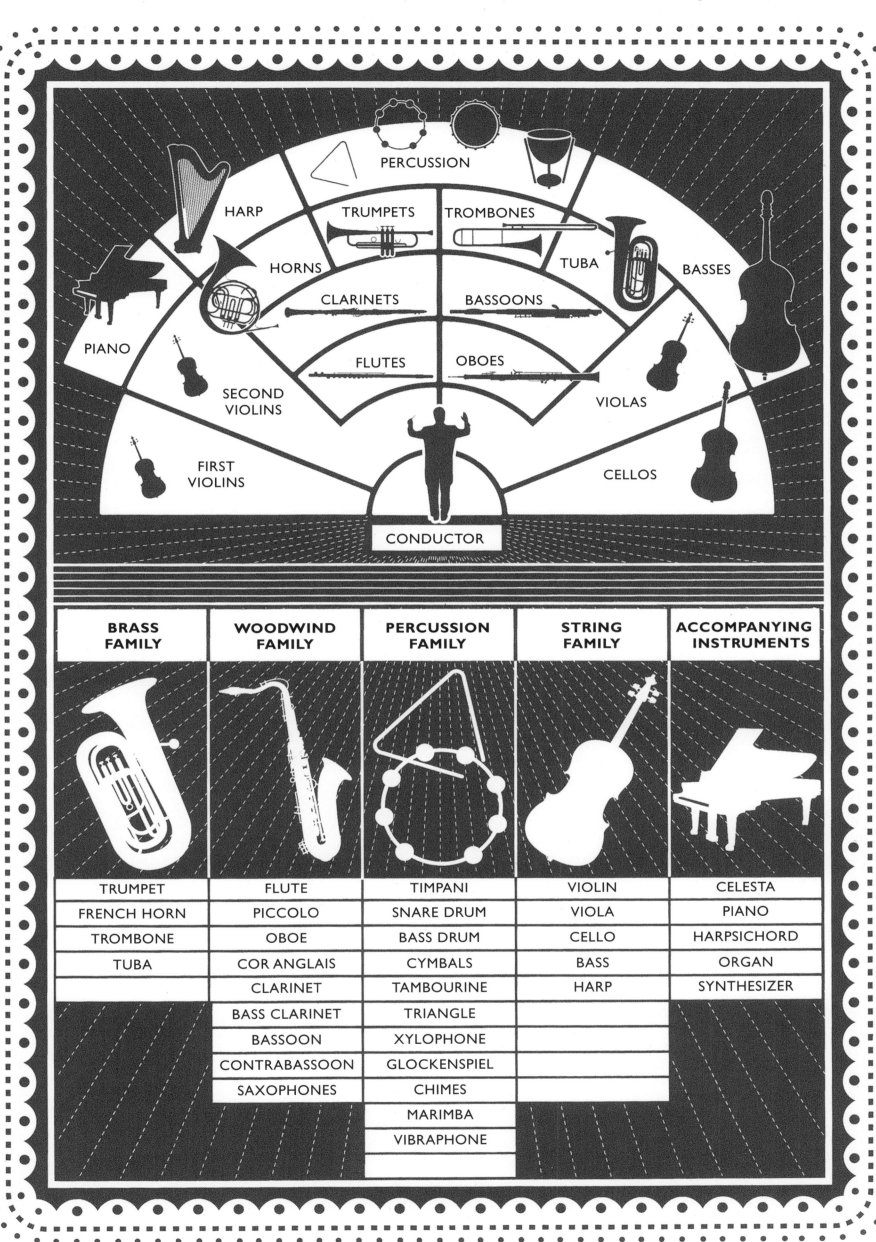

PERCUSSION

HARP   TRUMPETS   TROMBONES

HORNS   TUBA   BASSES

CLARINETS   BASSOONS

PIANO   FLUTES   OBOES

SECOND VIOLINS   VIOLAS

FIRST VIOLINS   CELLOS

CONDUCTOR

BRASS FAMILY	WOODWIND FAMILY	PERCUSSION FAMILY	STRING FAMILY	ACCOMPANYING INSTRUMENTS
TRUMPET	FLUTE	TIMPANI	VIOLIN	CELESTA
FRENCH HORN	PICCOLO	SNARE DRUM	VIOLA	PIANO
TROMBONE	OBOE	BASS DRUM	CELLO	HARPSICHORD
TUBA	COR ANGLAIS	CYMBALS	BASS	ORGAN
	CLARINET	TAMBOURINE	HARP	SYNTHESIZER
	BASS CLARINET	TRIANGLE		
	BASSOON	XYLOPHONE		
	CONTRABASSOON	GLOCKENSPIEL		
	SAXOPHONES	CHIMES		
		MARIMBA		
		VIBRAPHONE		

NEAP & SPRING
TIDES

A day at the beach offers a swift lesson on the tides: the water chases you up the sand, then retreats. But careful study shows that the height and timing of tides follow a lunar cycle.

WHAT, NO TIDE?

There are places where the tides hardly move. Enclosed seas such as the Mediterranean are obvious examples, but there are others in the middle of the great oceans. For example, the Pacific surrounds the island of Tahiti, but there is almost no tide there.

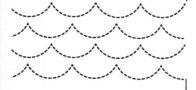

FIRST TIDE TABLE

About 2,200 years ago, Greek geographers recorded the tides, but the Chinese were the first to use their observations to predict the rise and fall: in 1056 they produced a tide table for the Fuchun River.

CAESAR'S MISTAKE

The tides almost wrecked the Roman invasion of England. Julius Caesar's troops were used to the Mediterranean, where the sea level barely changes. They crossed from France and moored their boats at low tide close to the sea. The tide — which often rises 20 feet on the English shore — almost swept them away.

The power and pulse of the tides are obvious to anyone visiting the coast. Ancient people could only wonder at their origin: according to legend in China and India, a great sea monster breathed the tides in and out.

Tidal rhythms are different on every beach, but typically the tide will rise and fall twice in a single day, then repeat the trick three-quarters of an hour later the next day.

The gravity of the moon and sun regulate the tides, pulling up a "lump" of water on the side of the earth they face. A second lump bulges on the far side. Both sweep around the oceans as the earth spins. If the sun's gravity alone pulled on the water, high tides would be half a day apart. However, the moon's pull complicates the picture. Because it orbits the earth every 29.5 (see pages 49–50) days, high tide arrives later each day.

Dragging the earth's oceans around also pushes the moon farther away — but only by 1.5 inches a year.

Spring tides occur twice a month, regardless of the season: they are named because they spring up and move quickly.

HOW DEEP IS THE WATER?

The sun and moon also affect the size of the tide. The tides are highest and lowest when the sun and moon line up (at a new moon) or when they are on opposite sides of the earth (at a full moon). This maximum tidal range is called a *spring tide*. One week after these spring tides (at a half moon), the gravity of the sun and moon oppose each other, and the resulting *neap tide* will neither rise nor fall as far.

That would be the end of the story if the oceans were very deep and every beach was a tiny island. However, ocean basins are relatively shallow, and friction with the seabed slows tidal flow. The shape of the continents also channels the moving water so that certain coasts have exceptionally high and low tides. Canada's Bay of Fundy takes the record, with a tidal range (high minus low) of more than 50 feet.

So many factors affect the tides that forecasting them accurately is fiendishly difficult. Computers cracked the problem: the first were mechanical and performed just this one task. Made of brass, they weighed many tons. Today the phone in your pocket can perform these calculations far faster and with greater precision.

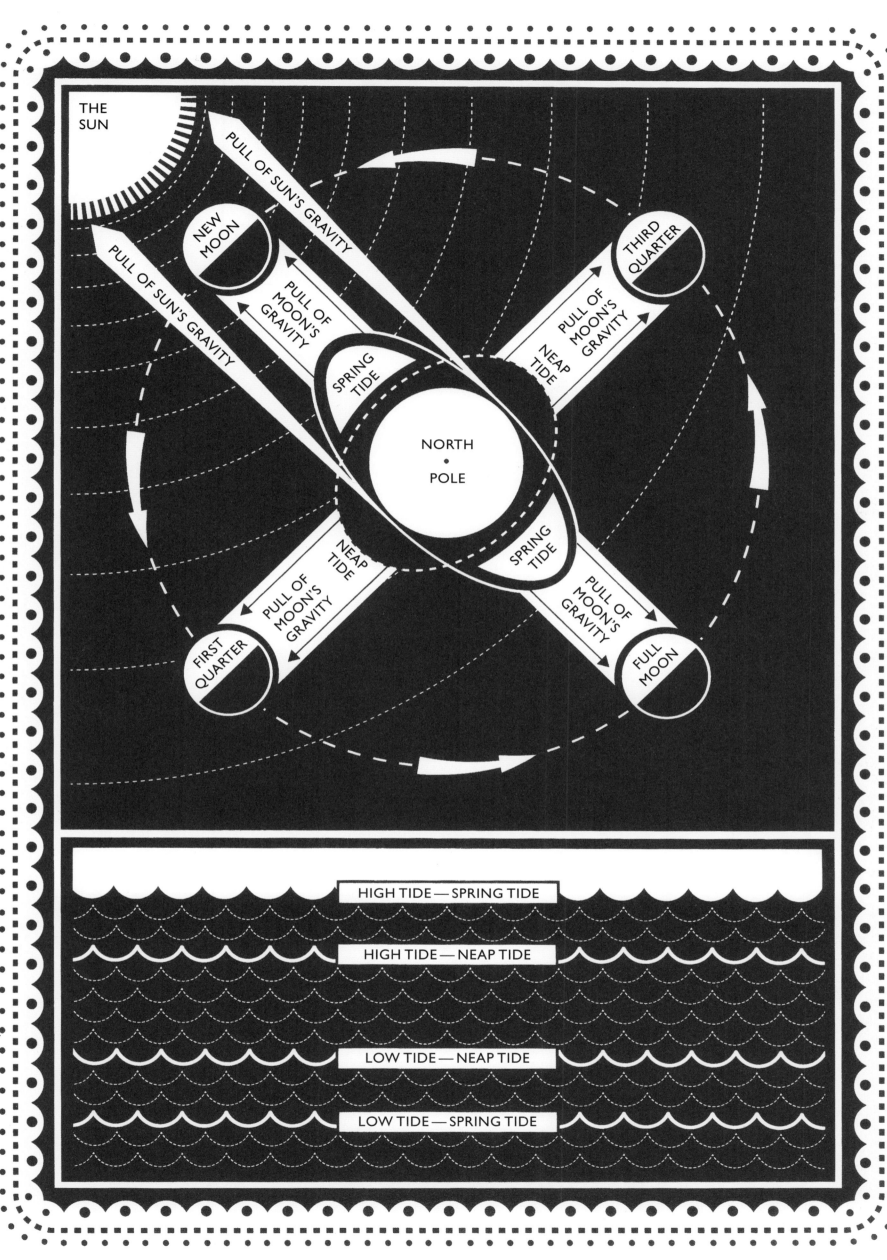

THE SUN

PULL OF SUN'S GRAVITY

PULL OF SUN'S GRAVITY

NEW MOON

THIRD QUARTER

PULL OF MOON'S GRAVITY

PULL OF MOON'S GRAVITY

SPRING TIDE

NEAP TIDE

NORTH POLE

NEAP TIDE

SPRING TIDE

FIRST QUARTER

PULL OF MOON'S GRAVITY

PULL OF MOON'S GRAVITY

FULL MOON

HIGH TIDE — SPRING TIDE

HIGH TIDE — NEAP TIDE

LOW TIDE — NEAP TIDE

LOW TIDE — SPRING TIDE

ROMAN NUMERALS

As soon as people began to have more than a couple of belongings, counting and recording numbers became a valuable skill. Roman numerals such as I, V, X, C, and D came directly from prehistoric methods of tallying.

I   II   III   IV   V   VI   VII   VIII   IX   X   XI   XII

The V of a Roman 5 is the top half of an X — the Roman 10.

The very earliest written numbers were knife cuts, or tallies, in wooden sticks. A single notch represented numeral 1; bigger numbers needed double nicks. Prehistoric farmers probably used sticks like these to count up their flocks and herds.

When the people of ancient Rome began recording numbers more than 2,500 years ago, they chose signs that resembled these straight knife cuts. With just a few quick nicks, they could record any number up to 89. For 1,000, Romans marked a symbol that looked like the Greek letter *phi*: Φ. "D" for 500 was the right-hand half of 1,000. "M" came into use in the Middle Ages (CE 1000–1500), perhaps as it was the first letter of *mille,* the Latin word for one thousand.

HARDER TO CHEAT
Bankers claimed Arabic numbers were easy to forge: a fourteenth-century Venetian book about accountancy argued "one can with ease make one [Arabic number] out of another, such as turning the zero into a 6 or a 9."

CHINESE NUMBERS
From about 400 BCE, Chinese people wrote numbers as groups of straight brush-strokes. These represented the counting rods that they placed on squared tables to add numbers, much as the Romans did.

A TABLE FOR SUMS
The Roman way worked well enough as a counting system, but it made arithmetic difficult. You couldn't just make a column of numbers, as we do now, and add first ones, then tens, and so on. For sums, the Romans used a counting board marked with lines separating thousands, hundreds, tens, and ones. They moved discs (called counters) over the board to symbolize the numbers they were adding.

INVENTING ZERO
The modern numbers that replaced the Roman system were first used in India around CE 500. They reached Europe indirectly, through the Middle East, so we call them Arabic numbers. What was especially clever about them was that they had a number for zero, which Roman numerals did not. Zero separated columns of figures, so that if a number had no hundreds, a zero kept an empty place in the hundreds column. This innovation made all the columns line up, greatly simplifying sums.

Though Arabic numbers now seem much easier to use, people in Europe at first found it hard to grasp the concept of a number that meant nothing. They clung to the Roman system, and it was not until the seventeenth century that 0 to 9 completely replaced the I, V, and X.

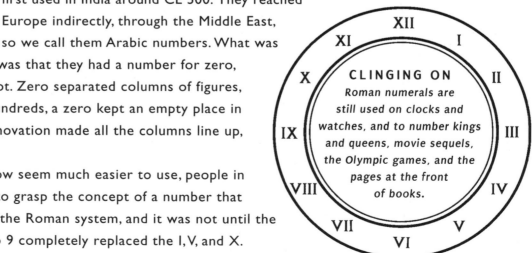

CLINGING ON
Roman numerals are still used on clocks and watches, and to number kings and queens, movie sequels, the Olympic games, and the pages at the front of books.

I V X L

| ONE | FIVE | TEN | FIFTY |

C D M

| ONE HUNDRED | FIVE HUNDRED | ONE THOUSAND |

I	1	XXI	21	XLI	41	LXI	61	LXXXI	81
II	2	XXII	22	XLII	42	LXII	62	LXXXII	82
III	3	XXIII	23	XLIII	43	LXIII	63	LXXXIII	83
IV	4	XXIV	24	XLIV	44	LXIV	64	LXXXIV	84
V	5	XXV	25	XLV	45	LXV	65	LXXXV	85
VI	6	XXVI	26	XLVI	46	LXVI	66	LXXXVI	86
VII	7	XXVII	27	XLVII	47	LXVII	67	LXXXVII	87
VIII	8	XXVIII	28	XLVIII	48	LXVIII	68	LXXXVIII	88
IX	9	XXIX	29	XLIX	49	LXIX	69	LXXXIX	89
X	10	XXX	30	L	50	LXX	70	XC	90
XI	11	XXXI	31	LI	51	LXXI	71	XCI	91
XII	12	XXXII	32	LII	52	LXXII	72	XCII	92
XIII	13	XXXIII	33	LIII	53	LXXIII	73	XCIII	93
XIV	14	XXXIV	34	LIV	54	LXXIV	74	XCIV	94
XV	15	XXXV	35	LV	55	LXXV	75	XCV	95
XVI	16	XXXVI	36	LVI	56	LXXVI	76	XCVI	96
XVII	17	XXXVII	37	LVII	57	LXXVII	77	XCVII	97
XVIII	18	XXXVIII	38	LVIII	58	LXXVIII	78	XCVIII	98
XIX	19	XXXIX	39	LIX	59	LXXIX	79	XCIX	99
XX	20	XL	40	LX	60	LXXX	80	C	100

THE MOHS SCALE
OF
MINERAL HARDNESS

Diamond or dud? True diamonds are so hard that they can't be marked and can easily scratch glass. "What-scratches-what" tests began as an ancient way to judge hardness, but German mineralogist Friedrich Mohs made them scientific.

ROCK COLLECTOR

Friedrich Mohs went to work for Austrian banker Jakob Friedrich van der Nüll. Despite his surname, which ironically means "zero" in German, Mohs's patron had huge wealth. He started collecting in 1797, and over ten years he bought eleven rock collections. With 4,000 specimens, his was the best collection in Germany.

HARDER THAN HARD

Scientists from the University of California at Berkeley predicted in 1985 that it should be possible to make a synthetic compound, beta carbon nitride, that would be harder than any natural material. Unfortunately, despite thirty years of trying, nobody has managed to make even the tiniest particles of it.

WHY IS DIAMOND SO HARD?

One of three forms of carbon, diamond is hard because each atom is in the middle of a tetrahedron (four-faced pyramid) of other atoms and is strongly bonded to each of them.

Roman naturalist Pliny the Elder had a keen interest in precious stones and their quality. Writing his encyclopedia *Natural History* in CE 77, he recommended comparison scratching to sort genuine stones from fakes. He added that "there is such a vast diversity in their degrees of hardness that some stones cannot be engraved with iron."

In the following centuries, prospectors, treasure hunters, and gem dealers relied on Pliny's wisdom. When geology began to emerge as a science in the seventeenth century, scratch testing was a rough-and-ready way of identifying all kinds of minerals.

MOHS TEST

The test we use today is named for its inventor, Friedrich Mohs, who devised it in 1822. He was working as a curator of rock samples in the collection of a rich banker, and his studies there led him to classify rocks by their physical qualities. One of these was hardness.

Mohs made a list of minerals in order of increasing hardness and numbered them from 1 to 10. In this way, Mohs defined hardness by ease of scratching. Each mineral could scratch the next one down in the scale, and could in turn be scratched only by a mineral of a higher ranking.

If you want to try Mohs's test, you can buy a kit of probes and plates to do it, but you can also make rough measurements with the simplest of tools. Your fingernail has a hardness of 2.5, a penny is 3.5, a steel nail 5.5, and the dull back of a porcelain tile is 6.5. If you wear a diamond ring, you can extend the scale all the way to 10.

THE LIMITS OF HARDNESS

The Mohs scale measures scratch resistance, but two more kinds of hardness have been identified since its invention: indentation hardness and rebound hardness. The first is tested by pressing the mineral with a sharp point until it leaves a dent. A strike from a hammer measures rebound hardness. All three kinds of testing are important in science and engineering. For instance, bendy metal dents easily, so indentation testing is a quick way to check the quality of steel parts such as pipes.

MOHS SCALE	SAMPLE MINERAL	APPEARANCE	SCRATCH TEST	ABSOLUTE HARDNESS
1	TALC		VERY EASILY SCRATCHED WITH A FINGERNAIL	1
2	GYPSUM		POSSIBLE TO SCRATCH WITH A FINGERNAIL	2
3	CALCITE		VERY EASILY SCRATCHED WITH A COPPER COIN	9
4	FLUORITE		VERY EASILY SCRATCHED WITH A KNIFE	21
5	APATITE	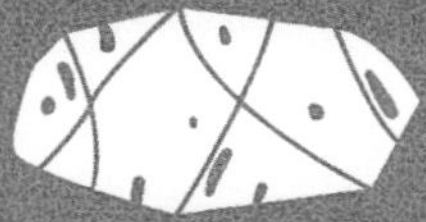	POSSIBLE TO SCRATCH WITH A KNIFE	48
6	ORTHOCLASE	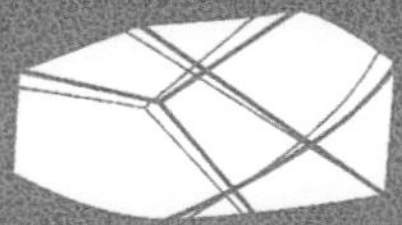	ONLY JUST SCRATCHES GLASS	72
7	QUARTZ	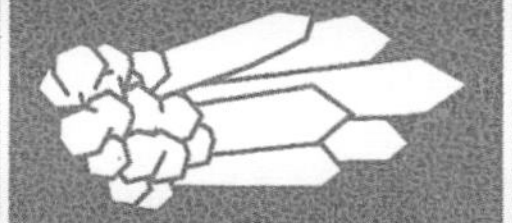	EASILY SCRATCHES GLASS	100
8	TOPAZ		VERY EASILY SCRATCHES GLASS	200
9	CORUNDUM		CUTS GLASS	400
10	DIAMOND	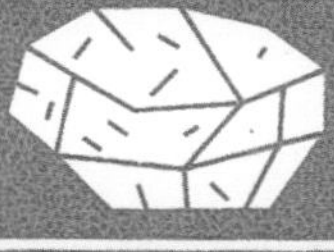	VERY EASILY CUTS GLASS	1,500

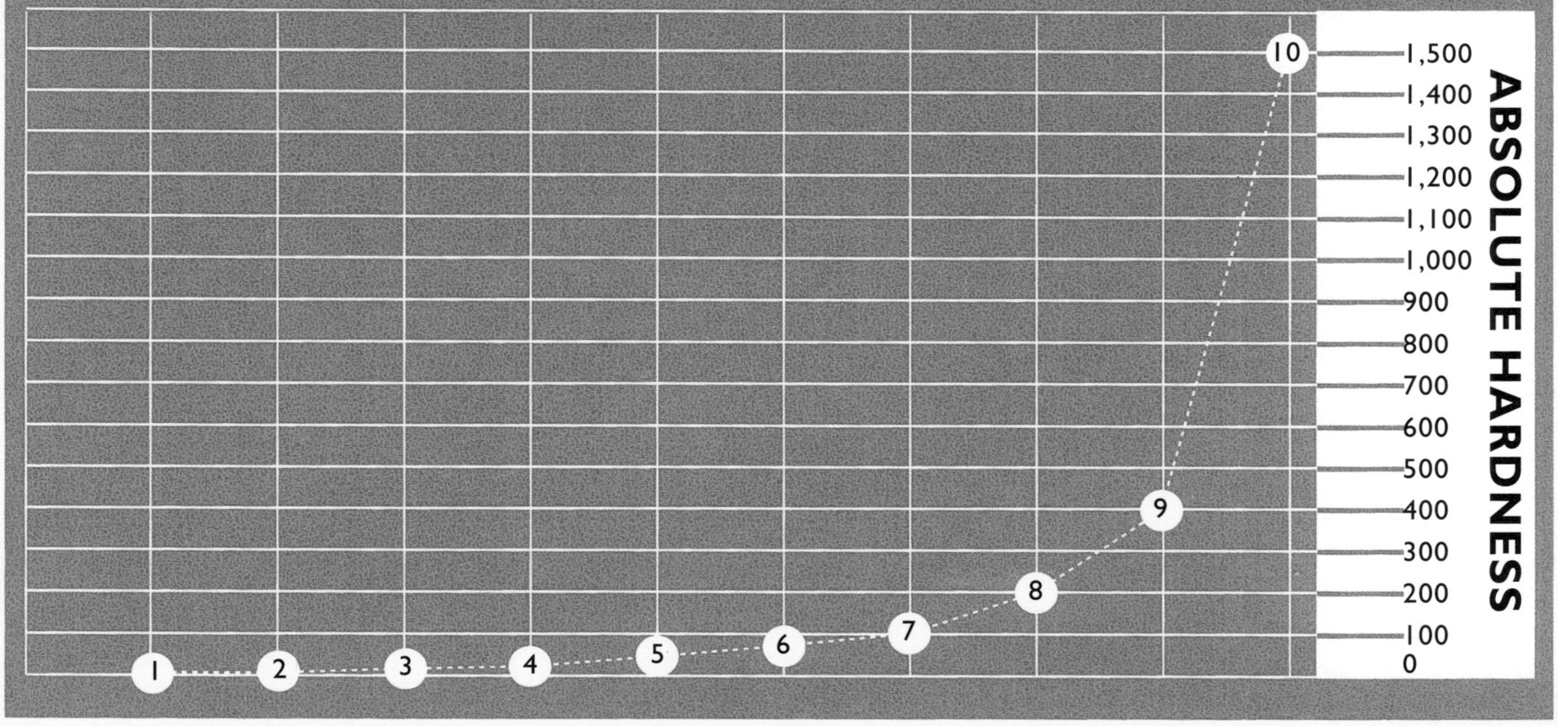

ABSOLUTE HARDNESS

1,500
1,400
1,300
1,200
1,100
1,000
900
800
700
600
500
400
300
200
100
0

INTERNATIONAL ORGANIZATION FOR STANDARDIZATION
PAPER SIZES

The very first sheets of paper were as big as the sieve-like trays on which they were molded. Cut into sheets for sale, paper came in a bewildering variety of sizes. Standard sizes ended the chaos only in the twentieth century.

ITALIAN LEADERS

Bologna had a paper mill as early as 1293, and city laws tried to establish standard sizes a century later. An engraved marble slab now in a Bologna museum shows the four permitted paper sizes: reçute, meçane, realle, and imperialle.

REVOLUTIONARY

A 1798 French law laid down paper sizes in which the width-to-height ratio is always the square root of 2, or 1.4142. Why pick this odd number? Because the proportions do not change if you cut the sheet in half with a paper knife or guillotine.

AN ARM'S LENGTH

There's a legend that the American letter size comes from the days when vatmen could not stretch their arms to hold a mold wider than 44 inches. When cut twice, the sheets they produced measured 11 inches.

From paper's invention in China in the third century, its manufacture by hand followed the same simple process everywhere. A "vatman" dipped a mold—wire mesh stretched on a frame—into a soupy pool of fibers. The water drained off, leaving paper sheets with ragged edges.

Paper merchants trimmed and cut these into smaller sheets for sale . . . in hundreds of different sizes. It was confusing and wasteful, and in 1398, the government of the Italian city of Bologna attempted to clear up the mess with the first standard sizes (see left).

The French began their own efforts after revolution rocked their country. The people's government wanted new standards for everything. They introduced the metric system of meters and kilograms, and a 1798 law set down a small range of permitted sizes of paper. *Grand registre,* the biggest sheet, was exactly the size of modern A2, one of the international standard metric sizes used everywhere except the United States and Canada.

The new law hardly improved things: French printers continued to use a chaotic range of sizes. It was the same in other countries: British paper merchants had names for nearly 290 sizes. Real standardization began only after 1922, when a German committee defined the modern metric A and B sizes. It was quickly adopted almost worldwide. But not quite.

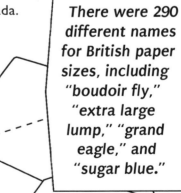

There were 290 different names for British paper sizes, including "boudoir fly," "extra large lump," "grand eagle," and "sugar blue."

AMERICA IS DIFFERENT

American paper, of course, is measured in inches: letter size is 8½ x 11. Nobody is quite sure where this format came from, but there were many more until the 1920s, when two government committees decided to standardize the letter format. At first, neither committee knew about the other. The Committee on the Simplification of Paper Sizes chose the letter size in use today, but the Permanent Conference on Printing chose 8 x 10½. When the two groups finally met to agree on a size, each stubbornly backed its chosen format. Both remained in use until President Reagan finally chose the modern standard, sixty years later.

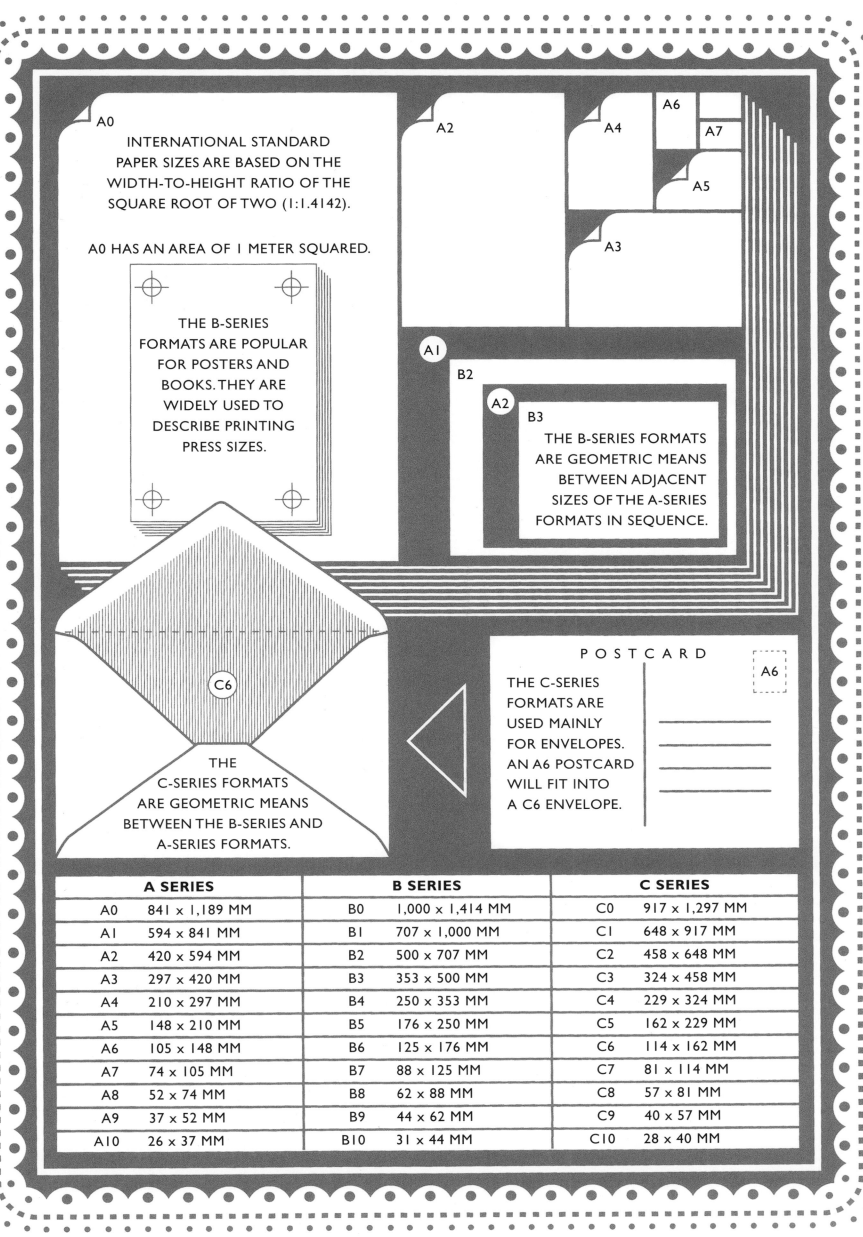

A0

INTERNATIONAL STANDARD PAPER SIZES ARE BASED ON THE WIDTH-TO-HEIGHT RATIO OF THE SQUARE ROOT OF TWO (1:1.4142).

A0 HAS AN AREA OF 1 METER SQUARED.

THE B-SERIES FORMATS ARE POPULAR FOR POSTERS AND BOOKS. THEY ARE WIDELY USED TO DESCRIBE PRINTING PRESS SIZES.

A2

A4

A6

A7

A5

A3

A1

B2

A2

B3

THE B-SERIES FORMATS ARE GEOMETRIC MEANS BETWEEN ADJACENT SIZES OF THE A-SERIES FORMATS IN SEQUENCE.

C6

THE C-SERIES FORMATS ARE GEOMETRIC MEANS BETWEEN THE B-SERIES AND A-SERIES FORMATS.

POSTCARD

A6

THE C-SERIES FORMATS ARE USED MAINLY FOR ENVELOPES. AN A6 POSTCARD WILL FIT INTO A C6 ENVELOPE.

A SERIES		B SERIES		C SERIES	
A0	841 x 1,189 MM	B0	1,000 x 1,414 MM	C0	917 x 1,297 MM
A1	594 x 841 MM	B1	707 x 1,000 MM	C1	648 x 917 MM
A2	420 x 594 MM	B2	500 x 707 MM	C2	458 x 648 MM
A3	297 x 420 MM	B3	353 x 500 MM	C3	324 x 458 MM
A4	210 x 297 MM	B4	250 x 353 MM	C4	229 x 324 MM
A5	148 x 210 MM	B5	176 x 250 MM	C5	162 x 229 MM
A6	105 x 148 MM	B6	125 x 176 MM	C6	114 x 162 MM
A7	74 x 105 MM	B7	88 x 125 MM	C7	81 x 114 MM
A8	52 x 74 MM	B8	62 x 88 MM	C8	57 x 81 MM
A9	37 x 52 MM	B9	44 x 62 MM	C9	40 x 57 MM
A10	26 x 37 MM	B10	31 x 44 MM	C10	28 x 40 MM

To Charlie and Tom
J. B.

*To Jilly and Liam. Grateful thanks to Marcus Weeks, for his
help on music, and Will Manners, of the University
of York, for his advice about bicycles.*
R. P.

Text copyright © 2016 by Richard Platt
Illustrations copyright © 2016 by James Brown

First U.S. edition 2017

Library of Congress Catalog Card Number pending
ISBN 978-0-7636-9348-0

17 18 19 20 21 22 CCP 10 9 8 7 6 5 4 3 2 1

Printed in Shenzhen, Guangdong, China

This book was typeset in Gill and Puritan.
The illustrations were screen-printed.

Candlewick Studio
an imprint of
Candlewick Press
99 Dover Street
Somerville, Massachusetts 02144

www.candlewickstudio.com